What Happened to Christopher

What Happened to Christopher

An American Family's Story of
Shaken Baby Syndrome

Ann-Janine Morey

With a Foreword by
M. Joan McDermott

Southern Illinois University Press
CARBONDALE AND EDWARDSVILLE

Printed in the United States of America
01   00   99   98   4   3   2   1

Library of Congress Cataloging-in-Publication Data
Morey, Ann-Janine.
    What happened to Christopher : an American
family's story of shaken baby syndrome / Ann-Janine
Morey ; with a foreword by M. Joan McDermott.
      p.   cm.
    Includes bibliographical references.
     1. Attig, Christopher Michael. 2. Infanticide—
United States—Case studies. 3. Battered child
syndrome—United States—Case studies. I. Title.
HV6541.U6M67 1998
364. 15'23—DC21   98-5368
ISBN 0-8093-2215-3   CIP

The paper used in this publication meets the minimum
requirements of American National Standard for
Information Sciences—Permanence of Paper for Printed
Library Materials, ANSI Z39.48-1984. ∞

For
Gabriel Todd and Lucia Rose

I can tell you about
his soft cheeks, his little sing-song voice,
the way he danced around, how sweet his head smelled.
His jacket hangs on the bedroom door. He was the
best thing that ever happened to me.

Christopher Michael Attig
December 7, 1992–August 4, 1994

Contents

Foreword

hristopher Michael Attig was a "shining child," a normal, happy toddler who ran, played, cuddled, cried, and sat on Santa's lap. And he was still that shining child when he was shaken to death by Gary Gould, a man he loved and trusted. Ann-Janine Morey served as a jury alternate in Gould's trial. In *What Happened to Christopher*, she weaves together findings from research on shaken baby deaths, court records, and interviews with Christopher's family and criminal justice, medical, and other professionals.

As I read this book about Christopher's life and death, a causal mode of thinking clicked in, and I searched the book for reasons, for events that might have signaled danger, and for people and institutions to blame. Then at the end, I emerged sad and angry, convinced that Christopher's death should not have happened but at a loss in naming any one, single thing that might have prevented it.

Ann-Janine Morey wrote *What Happened to Christopher* to pay tribute to Christopher, to educate readers about Shaken Baby Syndrome, and to describe the harrowing aftermath for immediate and extended family when a child is killed. But she walks a tightrope here: writing about what led to Christopher's death, but not blaming his caretakers; writing about his family's grief, without concurring that retribution is essential; writing about what happened to Christopher, without an interview with Gary Gould; retelling the memories of family members, without questioning their validity. In this book, Morey is an advocate, an educator, and a representative of a family torn by tragedy.

This foreword, then, is written to enable readers to step back and consider the people and events in *What Happened to Christopher* within the broader framework of what we know about intimate violence. Here I am using the terms "intimate violence" and "family violence" interchangeably to refer to acts or omissions carried out intentionally (that is, not accidentally) to cause pain or injury to a family member or intimate. In addition, although also an advocate, I don't represent Christopher's family, and therefore I can make observations that Ann-Janine Morey might be unwilling to make.

Contexts and Causes

Two basic premises provide a context for understanding what happened to Christopher:

  1. Love and violence coexist in relationships.
  2. Inequality breeds violence.

One of the biggest obstacles to understanding family violence is the belief that love and violence can't coexist, that we can't care for people who hurt us and we can't hurt people who care for us. Yet reality contradicts this belief, again and again, through an array of intimate relationships. Women love men who beat them. Parents neglect and willfully harm children they love. Children terrorize their younger, weaker siblings, and teenagers assault their mothers and fathers. Adult caretakers, often women, abuse elderly parents.

In and around Christopher's life, too, love and violence were interwoven. Christopher's mother, Rhonda Carter, was attracted to men who treated her badly. Both of Christopher's grandmothers (Ruth Attig and Joyce Lockhart) were suspicious of Gary but, for love-related reasons, hesitant to intervene. So it *is* possible that Gary Gould — Gary the drug-using, drug-dealing, macho biker who allegedly assaulted Rhonda and killed her son — loved Christopher.

The second premise is that inequality in intimate relationships, mirroring broad patterns of inequality in society, produces violence. Noted family violence researcher David Gil believes that the inherent power differential between parents and children sets the stage for violence against children, just as it has been posited that gender inequality is the root of violence against women. Put simply, people hurt others because they can.

Risk Factors

If love and violence are intermingled in all of our lives, and many people are affected by patterns of social inequality, why are some children more likely than others to be hurt by their caretakers?

Ola W. Barnett, Cindy L. Miller-Perrin, and Robin D. Perrin have recently summarized "risk factors" identified in research as associated with physical child abuse, factors that they group into four categories: (1) offender characteristics, psychological or biological; (2) factors associated with the parent-child relationship; (3) characteristics of the family or family environment; and (4) situational and societal conditions.

Research comparing abusive to nonabusive parents shows links between certain individual characteristics and the propensity to abuse children. According to Barnett, Miller-Perrin, and Perrin, perpetrator characteristics include anger and anger control problems, depression, low frustration tolerance, low self-esteem, rigidity, deficits in empathy, substance abuse or dependence, physical health problems, and physiological reactivity. Child abuse offenders are described by other researchers (Bolton and Bolton) as being immature, having needs for domination and control, approving the use of violence, and lacking preparation for family roles.

Parent-child relationship factors that place children at risk can be characteristics of the child or the parent. At greater risk of being abused are young children and those with difficult behaviors or with physical or mental disabilities. These are the weaker, more vulnerable children and those who pose special parenting challenges or place greater than average demands on caretakers. By contrast, parents at risk of abusing their children have poor parenting skills and unrealistic, often age-inappropriate, expectations of children. They may also have negative perceptions about child rearing or think that parenting is stressful. Anyone who has lost his or her temper with a young child can see deadly potential in the combination of difficult children and stressed, ill-equipped parents.

The third set of risk factors includes characteristics of families. Child abuse is more likely to occur in families with current abuse practices (for example, spouse abuse), families with intergenerational patterns of abuse (that is, a parent was abused as a child), families with marital problems, or families that generally show few positive parent-child interactions and many critical or controlling interactions.

The fourth set of risk factors for child abuse identified by Barnett and her colleagues contains both situational and societal conditions. The situational factors include problematic living arrangements such as low socioeconomic status, single-parent households, public assistance, unemployment or part-time work, situational stress, and social isolation.

Controversy exists in the research literature about the relationships between child abuse and certain of these attributes, such as low socio-economic status. Research on the characteristics of abusers is most often conducted using officially reported cases, and the argument is that lower-income individuals are more likely to be reported for child abuse, while middle- and upper-class perpetrators escape detection. There is, however, more support for the position taken here, which is that while child abuse occurs in families at all income levels, it is more likely to occur in situations in which poverty or economic instability produces stressful living arrangements and family relations.

Certain societal-level variables are also included in the fourth set of risk factors. Child abuse is more likely to occur in societies that generally approve of violence and, specifically, condone corporal punishment. Other societal factors associated with child abuse are those related to power imbalances, as noted earlier. That is, child abuse is more likely when there are strong power differentials in society and in the family.

Which of these risk factors were present in Christopher's case?

First, consider perpetrator characteristics. Gary Gould was not interviewed, so we don't know much about him. He is described as quick to anger and self-centered (about Christopher's death Gary says, "It's the worst thing that's happened to me in my life"), as lacking direction and intermittently employed, and as a man who used and abused illegal drugs and alcohol. He's a small-town tough-guy with a rural, southern readiness to use violence as a response to a wide range of conflict situations. The Gary we learn about through Ann-Janine Morey's interviews has too much testosterone and too little stability to be minding a sick little boy.

Second, consider risk factors associated with Christopher himself. The child was a toddler. The morning he was assaulted, he was restless and whining, probably from an ear infection.

Next, think about factors in the family environment. In some families, violence is repeated over generations, as if victims act with complicity in learned patterns of assaultive relationships. (This is why it is always tempting to blame the victims of family violence.) Rhonda, like her mother, was no stranger to intimate violence. She was assaulted by Chuck Attig, her ex-husband, when she was pregnant, and she was allegedly raped by Gary. We also get the sense that Rhonda was drawn to aggressive, domineering, macho men, men with criminal histories and rigid ideas about gender roles. Violence, inequality, and instability characterized Rhonda's relationships with men, unhealthy relationships for Rhonda and for her son.

Rhonda is not the villain here, but her irresponsibility invites our criticism. Was Rhonda more concerned with her own good times than the welfare of her son? Or, was Rhonda a reasonably competent mother but a victim of bad judgment? Should she have been able to predict what would happen on that hot and humid summer morning?

Finally, add to this troublesome mix some of the situational factors noted above. Certainly, Rhonda's economic situation was tenuous at best. The stress of caring for Christopher, with the constant shuffling of responsibility for the child among family members, was wearing on everybody. Christopher's grandparents were justified in their worry over this instability, this precariousness. Who *was* taking care of Christopher?

Offender, child, family, and situational risk factors were abundant in Christopher's life and in the lives of his extended family. Perhaps Judge David W. Watt was right: "He never had a chance outside of his grandparents."

Beyond Causes

By definition, individual case studies offer at best a partial understanding of causation. And, as much as we learn from *What Happened to Christopher*, there's too much we don't know, especially about Gary Gould. More important, picking apart Christopher's story for causes of child abuse comes too close to blaming the victims—his family—for his death, a devastating blame they already feel intensely. The value of adding Christopher's story to the growing literature on SBS does not lie in causal analysis. Rather, his case adds depth and dimension to our understanding. Family violence is as messy and full of contradictions as life itself.

We don't approve of Rhonda's drug use and partying, or her inability to provide a safe and stable home for her child. Still, Rhonda loved her son. Who grows into adulthood without feeling invulnerable, craving excitement, and seeking attention? So, while we can't bring ourselves to absolve "free spirit" Rhonda, we also know it isn't our place to do so. We understand how she could leave her sick son with Gary Gould, just as we are sympathetic with the grandmothers who were hesitant to interfere.

Grief and Punishment

"This was his home," both grandmothers said. *What Happened to Christopher* is as much about the rippling and debilitating consequences of violent child death as it is about SBS. Ann-Janine Morey respects grief. While unfeeling friends and acquaintances of both grandmothers complain that their grief is excessive, Morey flounders, just like Ruth, Joyce, and the rest of us, in suggesting ways to cope with the violent death of a child. Belief in God? A criminal conviction?

A terrible truth about punishment is that retribution fails to heal. Victims who are able to forgive offenders do experience relief. However, practices of restorative justice — efforts to bring together victims and offenders to fashion reconciliation and peace — are infrequently thought of in connection with intimate violence because of the concern with victim protection. For example, marital counseling is frowned upon by advocates for battered women who see too much potential for returning to relationships imbalanced in power and likely to produce repeat victimization.

Christopher's family faults the legal system for protecting the offender at the expense of helping the victims, and they're not alone in their thinking. The criminal justice system has long been criticized for its neglect of victims. Only in the past few decades has the victims' rights movement accomplished significant change in the way victims are treated by the system. It is also fair to say that the criminal law and the criminal justice system are better at responding to violence perpetrated by strangers, even though the sad irony is that individuals are more likely to be hurt by persons they know.

I think victims' feelings of helplessness and frustration in the face of child death are intensified in cases like Christopher's. When the perpetrator is a caretaker, that is, when the crime is not the random act of a stranger, trust is violated. Households, lives, and relationships are damaged or destroyed.

Victims' rights advocates say that the blanket portrayal of crime victims as vengeful, conservative, and unforgiving is misleading. Victim advocate Anne K. Seymour explains that victims generally want two things: information and a chance to be believed and not blamed. She adds that crime prevention often becomes a major focus in the lives of crime victims.[1] All this is consistent with Christopher's family — asking for information, wanting to be heard, working to prevent future cases of SBS.

Why, then, does Ruth Attig believe that the system let her down? Ruth, Ann-Janine Morey, Judge Watt, and State's Attorney Michael Wepsiec all believe that laws protecting children should be tougher. Americans have a tendency to want to equate amount of concern about crime with amount of punishment — harsher laws indicate a problem is being taken seriously. Child endangerment laws might be strengthened, according to Wepsiec. For Judge Watt, the problem is the discrepancy in sentencing alternatives between manslaughter and murder.

We need to ask, Would a stiffer penalty for Gary really have made it easier for Christopher's family? What is the purpose of punishment in crimes such as this? Would tougher penalties deter potential violators in the future? Do we expect that a longer prison sentence will rehabilitate Gary but a shorter one won't? Do we believe that the Illinois Department of Corrections is reforming Gary Gould? Or, is Ruth Attig seeking retribution, payback, a balancing of harm and harm, an eye for an eye?

---

1. From Anne K. Seymour's presentation at the Justice Without Violence Conference, Albany, New York, June 1997.

I raise these questions with awareness of the tragedy of child death and great sympathy for Christopher's parents and extended family. Even so, I don't believe that the answer to violence is more violence. Over the centuries, countless volumes have been written debating the purposes of punishment and seeking to reconcile justice for the victim, for the offender, and for the community. These complicated questions are made more difficult when violence occurs in intimate relationships. Certainly, the deterrence argument has been made and has some validity — one of the reasons family violence is so common is that the consequences are minimal. On the other hand, is an irresponsible or immature caretaker likely to reason through the consequences of his or her behavior?

In some ways it is easier to forgive a stranger than an intimate. Nasty divorce wars and custody battles demonstrate the animosity that can develop between intimates. To end violence, though, we need to think about reintegrating offenders into their communities, and this means forgiveness. What's going to happen when Gary Gould is released, soon, to return home to Murphysboro?

Intervention and Prevention

Physical child abuse, like other types of family violence, is a complex phenomenon, with medical, legal, social, and psychological aspects. In addressing the problem of SBS, we need to consider all of these dimensions. While the diagnosis of SBS has become easier with advances in medical technology such as computed tomographic (CT) scanning and magnetic resonance imaging (MRI), medical experts still tell us that child abuse often becomes a "diagnosis of exclusion"; that is, an official report of child abuse is only filed "after rarer, but more 'acceptable' diagnoses are ruled out."[2]

2. Elaine M. Billmire and Patricia A. Myers, "Serious Head Injury in Infants: Accident or Abuse," *Pediatrics* 75 (1985): 340.

Even when diagnosed and reported, SBS is not easily prosecuted under existing laws, as Christopher's story reveals. For the criminal law, the criminal justice system, and even for the child protection system, shaken baby deaths are not business as usual. Research data show that child abuse, not accidents, is the most common cause of serious head injury to children under the age of one.[3] But if Christopher's story tells us anything about SBS in the courtroom, it tells us that juries are incapable of or unwilling to recognize a high degree of criminal intent in SBS. More startling to SBS advocates is the recent, internationally publicized Massachusetts trial of the British au pair, in which the judge overturned the jury's verdict, reducing the conviction from second degree murder to involuntary manslaughter and the sentence from life to time served (about nine months).

Several studies conducted between 1982 and 1990 showed that between 25 and 50 percent of teenagers and adults did not know that shaking a baby is dangerous.[4] For both Ann-Janine Morey and Christopher Attig's family, public education is key in the design of strategies to prevent shaken baby deaths. I agree. Also necessary are changes in law and policy to allow the criminal justice, child welfare, health, and mental health systems to respond effectively and in collaboration when child abuse does occur.

Much has been written on specific tactics to combat child abuse, and more generally, intimate violence. On the topic of "what to do" to prevent family violence we are not ignorant. However, spanking, slapping, and hitting children are still commonly accepted forms of discipline in our society. The research cited by Barnett, Miller-Perrin, and Perrin indicates that 90 percent of parents use some form of physical punishment on their children, and more than nine out of ten young

---

3. Billmire and Myers, 340.

4. Jacy Showers, "Shaken Baby Syndrome: The Problem and a Model for Prevention," *Children Today* 21 (1992): n 2.

adults report experiencing some physical punishment as children and adolescents. Findings such as these suggest a high degree of tolerance for violence in intimate relationships. What messages do children receive when parents use physical discipline to gain the upper hand?

In the end, *What Happened to Christopher* tells us this: To eliminate family violence, we must as individuals eliminate violence and inequality in our lives. As parents, teachers, students, child welfare or health professionals, as ordinary citizens leading ordinary lives, we need to reflect on (and maybe change) our own attitudes and behaviors. We must look within ourselves for the seeds of violence — tolerance or support of gender, class, race, and other types of social inequality. If we believe men should be powerful and women submissive, if we believe that parents are generally justified in using violence to discipline, if we continue to pretend that all the Rhondas and Chucks and Garys are different from ourselves, then we will never solve the problem of family violence.

We owe a debt of gratitude to Christopher's family for letting us into their lives, not because they are different, but because their lives and inequalities are ours. Until we are all willing to commit ourselves to eliminating violence, we won't escape the grieving.

M. Joan McDermott
Center for the Study of Crime, Delinquency, and Corrections
Southern Illinois University at Carbondale

Acknowledgments

This is a story about ordinary people whose lives have been permanently altered by the death of a child. What is not typical or ordinary, I think, is the courage with which Christopher's family has addressed his death. All members have been generous with their time and memories, both during the interviewing process and in the succeeding months in which I wrote the book. They talked with me out of love for Christopher, and it is their hope that by telling his story, they can spare another family this kind of suffering.

I have used pseudonyms to afford greater privacy for some persons who disclosed information that might be embarrassing to themselves or to others, to protect the identity of minors, and for some persons whose speech and actions are part of the public record but were not part of my interviewing. In a few instances, I have reconstructed dialogue based upon legal records and witness reports that detail the witnesses' speech, thoughts, and actions and what they witnessed or understood to be the speech, thoughts, or actions of others. Gary Gould did not respond to requests for an interview.

I owe a great debt to a number of people who encouraged and supported this project along the way. Provost Dr. John S. Jackson, then dean of the College of Liberal Arts at Southern Illinois University at Carbondale, with the cooperation of Vera Slankard, made it possible for me to hire someone to transcribe interview tapes. That someone, Allison Owen, spent a lonely summer cooped up in my office, filling her ears with someone else's grief. Brenda Yucas and Julia Galbus transcribed the last of the interview tapes. Court transcriber Sarah Justice

Hinde, Jackson County State's Attorney Michael Wepsiec, and Assistant State's Attorney Sheila Simon made negotiating the legal system much easier for a novice, and Carolyn Donow did the same for me relative to SIUC's internal fellowship system. Dr. Benjamin A. Shepherd, then provost of SIUC, funded my trip to Salt Lake City for the first National Conference on Shaken Baby Syndrome. Dr. Michael Graham and Dr. Bruce Kaufman graciously responded to my questions and helped me improve my accuracy in explaining some of the medical aspects of Shaken Baby Syndrome. Any shortcomings in my explanations are, of course, my responsibility. Dr. Jacy Showers, Stacy Iverson, and Dr. M. E. B. Phillips offered timely information and insights about SBS and organizations dedicated to eradicating child abuse. Mary Taylor, medical reference librarian at SIUC, rescued me more than once by locating key resources. A Special Projects Research Fellowship through SIUC's Office of Research and Development brought me both supporting research materials and the cheerful efficiency of research assistants Julia Galbus and Wendy Kautz. To all, I am most grateful.

Members of Christopher's family were given an opportunity to read the first draft of the manuscript. It was not easy for them to relive these events in print, nor to see how the story looked through someone else's eyes. I am indebted to them for taking the time to respond to the manuscript. The insights and experiences of Roger Smith, Jay Lewis, Melody Chamberlin, Chris Doerr, Sheila Simon, Michael Wepsiec, Judge David W. Watt, and Dr. Dennis Klass also enriched my understanding of the many dimensions to Christopher's story. In addition, friendly critical readers and listeners helped me keep perspective: Jay Lewis, Mike Wepsiec, Beth Lordan, Brenda Yucas, Rev. Suzanne Webb, Carolyn Curtin Alessio, Henry Carrigan, Dr. Joan McDermott, Ron and Donna Hedinger, and Dr. Lisa Knopp and her students in the fall 1995 nonfiction prose writing class. The rigorous advice of Southern Illinois University Press editor John Wilson, Assistant Director Susan Wilson, and copyeditor Julie Bush helped me bring the manuscript to maturity. I am especially grateful to Rick Stetter, director of Southern Illinois University Press, for taking a chance with this book.

Without the loving and enthusiastic support of my husband, Todd Hedinger, I could not have written Christopher's story. I owe him and my children a great debt for their patience and devotion.

Finally, there is Ruth Attig, whose place in Christopher's short life far exceeded the usual role of grandmother. It was her voice that first caught the ear of my heart. This is not to overlook the love and care of other relatives in his life—his maternal grandmother, Joyce Lockhart, or his uncles, Tim Attig and young Buddy Lockhart, or his aunt Robyn Carter. Christopher lived within an extended family system, with a number of relatives who filled in for Chuck and Rhonda in caring for him. But unlike Joyce, who works year-round, Ruth had a job that gave her more flexible hours and free weekends and summers, all of which she devoted to Christopher, both when he was alive and during the writing of this book. I am grateful to Ruth for her trust that I would be able to do justice to Christopher.

Introduction

SHAKEN BABY SYNDROME:

AN ORDINARY HORROR STORY

I n December 1994, Angela Rubin, then humanities librarian at Southern Illinois University's Morris Library, knowing about my emerging project on child death, sent me a memorial notice she had clipped from the *Southern Illinoisan*. "I found this very touching," she wrote to me. It was a picture of a little boy dressed in his Santa hat, surrounded by presents. Even in the grainy newsprint, his round face is glowing and eager, full of holiday anticipation. "In loving memory of our precious Christopher Michael Attig who would have been two years old today, Wednesday, December 7, 1994. Sadly missed, The Attig family and friends," read the accompanying text. I didn't know anything about this little boy and remember thinking that maybe he died of some childhood illness. I put the clipping in my growing file on child death, uncertain why I was keeping it but unwilling to throw it away.

I continued my scholarly work on a new project, a study of women's literary representations of child death, and I began anticipating my sabbatical by reviewing and collecting the range of fictional and academic sources I would need to develop my project.

Then in March 1995 I was called up for jury duty, something that had never happened to me. Reluctantly, I made room on my calendar, reasoning that since one week of my duty was during our spring break, it would be easy enough to improvise during the second week, when classes would again be in session. I was counting on either not getting selected or else serving for some brisk, one- or two-day trial. I received lots of advice from friends and colleagues on how to evade my civic responsibility: dress like a hippie; tell them you believe everyone is guilty until proven innocent; act like a snotty professional woman. When I found out the upcoming trial was a murder case involving a young child, I confidently arranged my self-presentation: I was the mother of two young children (at that time, ages ten months and three and a half years) and I was doing academic work on child death. That should do it, I thought, and better yet, it was all true. I went to court dressed as myself and awaited release.

The bare facts of the case did nothing to change my certainty that I wanted out of my civic duty. A nineteen-month-old toddler named Christopher Michael Attig had suffered an inexplicable and fatal head injury while in the care of a man named Gary Lynn Gould. Gould was charged with first degree murder and involuntary manslaughter. This was all I heard on the first day of jury selection, but it was enough. As the jury selection proceeded, the names of other key persons surfaced: Rhonda Carter, his mother; Chuck Attig, his father; and his grandmothers, Joyce Lockhart and Ruth Attig. I hadn't heard of any of these people, and I didn't remember newspaper stories about the case. Stories about harm to children weren't high on my list of breakfast reading material.

As it turns out, violent child death is not something any of us wants to think about, and understandably so. Does anyone recall the opening scene of the movie version of Stephen King's *Pet Sematary*? Here is what I remember, which is enough to prevent me from renting the movie to check up on my own accuracy. A family is enjoying a picnic and hike in a meadow. The round, happy baby crawls away from the group and with the lightning speed of a newly mobile child heads toward the nearby highway. As the distance between the exuberant child and the unaware family group grows, as distance between the fast-moving truck traffic and the baby diminishes, we can only stiffen in horror and disbelief. And because it is Stephen King, our most gruesome, deadly fears become a vivid image upon the screen. Nothing stops the truck. Nothing stops the baby until the truck.

This, of course, is only the prelude for the horror story that follows, a tale set in motion by the overwhelming grief and guilt of the parents. Although King is often criticized for his extravagance and melodramatic prose, in this novel he has it right. The death of a child is a horror story all by itself. And then there is the grieving that follows, another kind of horror story. These are the proportions of grief that accompany the death of a child.

Even the thought of a child in danger is too much for most of us to contemplate. This is a crucial frontier for our civilized selves. For example, there isn't much in the way of human cravenness and fear that the entertainment industry doesn't exploit. Audiences enjoy seeing women treated in vicious, violent ways on the big screen, as witnessed by the perennial popularity of serial killer movies. But we draw the line at children. This may be, in part, a matter of practicality. It would be difficult, both ethically and legally, to ask toddler-age actors to participate in such stagings. But perhaps there is another reason as well, a sign that we are not totally depraved as a culture. I think audiences would revolt at being served up realistic spectacles of children being battered and killed. It's a plot line so unbearable as to be unmarketable.

Child killing is such an essential violation of trust and innocence that we turn away rather than confront the fear and pain of a brutalized child. How many of us found it impossible to think about, much less comprehend, the last moments of Susan Smith's young boys as they slowly drowned in the back seat of that car? Or Elisa Izquierdo, bludgeoned to death by her psychotic mother and then memorialized on the December 11, 1995, cover of *Time* magazine? Many of us simply snapped off the TV, shut down the radio, turned away in tears. What else could we do? Such deaths are intolerable. When child deaths are brought to our attention, we express the appropriate outrage, we demand an accounting. And then we sink safely back into our lives. We don't know what to do, and sometimes it just seems easier not to know about such ugly events, period. We think death by child abuse is a problem in some family remote from our own safe and happy life.

That's what I thought, at any rate.

I was in one of the last jury panels interviewed for the trial, and this made me even more confident that I would be disqualified. During this process of jury interview and selection, what is called the *voir dire*, the defense lawyer, Paul Christenson, launched a series of questions about my research topic, checking for possible bias. Although I had brought the matter up with the full intention of using my research as a reason for being disqualified for service, I found myself insulted at the idea that I could not function as an objective witness to the case before me. More ignobly, I was acting like many a passerby to the scene of an accident, proclaiming my disinterest in the gory details while standing on tiptoe to see what's going on. I finally responded to his questions by saying that my area of expertise was literary death, not real death, a fact that made academics seem, well, academic indeed.

I thought I was so well defended against jury service that when my name was called as an alternate juror, I can still remember the chill that came over me, whispering at my scalp. I was afraid of what lay ahead. I didn't want to have to think about this violent death, but my fear was doubly selfish. I also didn't want to find out just how decorative, as in useless, my life's work as a scholar had been.

By the end of the four-day trial, I knew I could not continue writing the book I had planned, for into my secure academic world flooded the grief and pain unleashed by the death of Christopher Attig. On the second day of the trial, I remembered the clipping Angela Rubin had sent me. Had that been the same child? I raced back to my office and rummaged frantically through my stacks of photocopied articles, scribbled notes, and sheets of library references. And then, there he was, dressed in his Santa hat, his face glowing and eager, lighting up my files, waiting to be recognized. Christopher Michael Attig. I have never been impressed with the fatedness of things before that moment, but as I stared in disbelief at the fragile clipping sent so many months before, I felt certain I was meant to be in that courtroom, hearing about the terrible thing that was done to this little boy.

I did not feel certain, however, that I was prepared for what I would hear. In the fiction I had studied, children die accidentally or from illness. Some of the accidental deaths in these literary portrayals could be attributed to parental negligence, but I had not turned up a fictional portrayal in which a parent or caretaker deliberately and coldly kills a child. As in the world of entertainment, this is one topic literary artists seem to have avoided.

Meanwhile, in real life, "deaths from abuse and neglect of children four and younger outnumber those from falls, choking on food, suffocation, accidental drownings, residential fires or car accidents."[1] In this age of family values rhetoric, it is shocking to learn that more than one million cases of child abuse or neglect were documented in the United States in 1994, although the actual number of mistreated children may be closer to 2.3 million. Of these million or so abused and neglected children, over two thousand of them die every year. That's five children who die every day of the year from brutality or neglect or both. Worse yet, *A Nation's Shame: Fatal Child Abuse and Neglect in the United States*, a comprehensive review and update from the U.S. Advisory Board on Child Abuse and Neglect published a year after Christopher Attig was killed, presents a horrifying fact: in 90 percent of the cases reported to state agencies, children were abused by parents (80 percent) or caretakers related to them (10 percent). That is, despite sensational news coverage of kidnappings and killings by menacing strangers, the leading cause of death for children under the age of four

1. U.S. Advisory Board on Child Abuse and Neglect, *A Nation's Shame: Fatal Child Abuse and Neglect in the United States* (Washington, DC: U.S. Department of Health and Human Services, 1995), xxv (hereafter cited in notes and in text as *A Nation's Shame*).

in the United States is violence at the hands of those who presumably have promised to love and cherish them.

Here are some of their bodies, laid out for us one after the other in *A Nation's Shame*:

> Jamiel Neal, age 3, severely battered and burned with a stun gun;
> Shayne Bryant, age 4, scalded and beaten;
> Jose Manuel Garcia, age 2, burned to death;
> Saraphina Johnson, age 5 months, shaken to death;
> Thomas Owenby, age 10 months, starved to death;
> Lindsay Creason, age 3 weeks, smothered to end crying;
> Cody James, age 19 months, forced Valium overdose;
> Latoya Harris, age 8, found entombed in cement;
> Michael Cecil, age 2, chronically battered to death;
> Richard Jones, age 1½, severe intoxication;
> Baby Girl Buchanan, age 3 months, starved to death;
> Daryl Bell, Jr., age 2, severely beaten after wetting pants;
> Eric Dunphy, age 2, severely beaten and stuffed into a Christmas ornament box;
> Kelly Jackson, age 4 months, shaken to death;
> Felicia Brown, age 1½, beaten with a shoe heel;
> Anonymous toddler, age 3, severely beaten after crying over fear of the dark.

These are the ordinary child abuse deaths that likely didn't make the nightly news, because only the really spectacular deaths are carried nationwide, the rest relegated to a brief note in the local paper, if that. There are many more where those came from, but on a daily basis, we are largely insulated from the terrifying reality so meticulously recorded in *A Nation's Shame*. For too many children, parents and caretakers are not a refuge from the terrors of the world; they have become the fearful, killing dark.

Before March of 1995, I didn't know any of these things. Even reading fictional accounts of child death scared me, as though I were endangering my own children by even thinking about the subject. I felt I was being brave simply by considering the topic, and through my academic writing, I felt I would do justice and my duty. I was wrong.

Although I tried, I could not walk away from what I'd seen and heard in that courtroom. I put my literature on the shelf, rededicated my sabbatical, and began looking for the story. I called Ruth Attig, Christopher's paternal grandmother, and asked her if she would talk to me about her grandson. Then, having heard too much to turn back, I contacted other members of Christopher's family.

There is no abuse death that is worse than any other. All are inexcusable, shameful testimony to adult immaturity and cruelty. I focus on Shaken Baby Syndrome (SBS) in this book because it is the death that invaded my life. It is, however, an especially insidious form of child abuse death, one that has recently become the subject of public awareness campaigns as our medical understanding of this form of abuse has grown.

SBS was described in 1972 and 1974 by pediatric radiologist John Caffey. In the years that have followed, other medical researchers have confirmed and enhanced Caffey's descriptions of what he called "whiplash shaken infant syndrome." According to Monteleone and Brodeur, SBS accounts for 50 percent of all nonaccidental injury done to children, and of any abuse injury, the aftereffects are the most severe (12). Why is this so?

The term "shaking" is misleading relative to the damage that results from this activity. When a caretaker shakes a child, he or she is doing so in rage, using excessive force. Most shaking injuries occur in children under the age of two, although there are documented cases of shaking injury and death up to age four. Two factors are critical in producing this injury. One is the difference in size between the attacker and the victim, and the other is a matter of infant physiology. A young child's head is overweight compared to the rest of his or her body, and the neck muscles are not yet strong enough to fully control the oversized head. In addition, the skull wall is still thin, and the brain is still growing. When a child is shaken, the head snaps back and forth violently. Inside the fixed walls of the skull, the brain slams repeatedly against the hard surface, bruising delicate tissue and tearing vital nerve connections. The brain swells and bleeds and in severe cases is unable to continue basic nervous system function. The child rapidly loses consciousness, vision, and finally the ability to breathe. The child who dies from SBS dies from massive cerebral swelling. The child who survives likely sustains a variety of permanent brain injuries including blindness, cerebral palsy, and cognitive and learning disabilities.

There are a constellation of injuries and presenting symptoms that medical personnel have learned to look for in SBS. These include retinal hemorrhages, closed head bleeding, skull fractures, coma, cerebrate posturing (stylized and rhythmic seizures), respiratory problems, convulsions, and external bruising. Of these, retinal hemorrhages are so closely associated with SBS that some physicians have called for routine examination of young babies' eyes as a form of early detection.

Confessions from convicted abusers tell us that the shaking that occurs is violent, lasting anywhere from ten to thirty seconds, although medical personnel are uneasy about ascribing too literal a time frame to the amount of time it takes to produce the injury. Those who have confessed are likely to minimize their actions. Researchers do agree on the amount of force necessary to produce the injury. According to the 1993 statement published by the American Academy of Pediatrics Committee on Child Abuse and Neglect, the shaking is so violent that "any competent individual observing the shaking would recognize it as dangerous" (872). In the case of a severe shaking, once the injuries have been inflicted, there is a rapid change in consciousness in the child, and experts agree that symptoms present almost immediately.[2]

This last medical item is important, because there are almost never witnesses to these injuries, which occur when the child is alone with the attacker. This is, literally, a way to kill a child using your bare hands, leaving little or seemingly inexplicable evidence behind. The method of attack is to grab the child by the shoulders or chest and shake violently. Sometimes there are telltale fingerprint bruises. One convicted assailant described grabbing the child by the feet and swinging and shaking that way. The injuries induced may be caused solely by shaking, or they may be compounded by impact injuries—throwing the child against a surface or hitting the child directly on the head. Only in the latter case is there immediate external evidence of trauma. Otherwise, shaken baby injuries may very well go undetected. The lethal damage is all hidden within the skull, which is why this type of injury is often referred to as a closed head injury. It is also why, until recently, this injury has been so difficult to detect. Researchers in this area suspect that the incidence of SBS may be grossly underreported or misclassified as Sudden Infant Death Syndrome (SIDS).

Because we have been looking more deeply into child abuse and SBS, we know something about the attackers, too. It is usually not mothers, although it may sometimes be the female baby-sitter. Typically, however, most physical abuse fatalities are caused by enraged or

2. Mary E. S. Case, "Head Injury in Child Abuse," in *Child Maltreatment: A Clinical Guide and Reference*, ed. James A. Monteleone and Armand E. Brodeur (St. Louis: G. W. Medical Publishing, 1994); Robert H. Kirschner and Harry L. Wilson, "Fatal Child Abuse: The Pathologist's Perspective," in *Child Abuse: Medical Diagnosis and Management*, ed. Robert M. Reece (Philadelphia: Lea & Febiger, 1994); Carolyn J. Levitt, Wilbur L. Smith, and Randell C. Alexander, "Abusive Head Trauma," in *Child Abuse: Medical Diagnosis and Management*, ed. Robert M. Reece (Philadelphia: Lea & Febiger, 1994).

extremely stressed fathers or other male caretakers, who outnumber abusive females two to one. This out-of-control male is usually in his mid-twenties, has no more than a high school education (if that), lives near poverty level, and copes poorly with stress. He may have experienced violence in his own life firsthand. Substance abuse is often implicated as well. According to *A Nation's Shame*, "these men primarily assault infants and very small children by beating their heads and bodies, shaking them violently, intentionally suffocating them, immersing them in scalding water, and performing other brutal acts" (13). In the case of SBS, the specific trigger for the attack is usually a child's inconsolable crying.

There's nothing controversial about child abuse. It's an easy soapbox platform, an issue guaranteed to unite a room full of people. And yet, as a society, it seems we are always found weeping at the graveyard, looking for an answer after the fact, demanding that someone, anyone, be more accountable so that we do not have to contemplate this kind of loss again. How can we respond more effectively?

Although there are no one-size-fits-all answers to a question like this, through this book, I offer a beginning point. Before we can prevent child abuse, we have to be willing to see it. Yes, we all find child abuse abhorrent, and yet, as I will discuss in a later chapter, it is one of the most difficult kinds of murders to prosecute successfully. Ironically, it seems that we find child abuse so awful that we cannot bear to think that any adult could do such a thing. The result of this nobility of sentiment is that child murders often go unprosecuted and child killers go unconvicted, or if they are convicted, we choose a lesser sentence. In the case of SBS, there is a tendency to offer leniency to the culprits on the grounds that they did not "intend" to do such harm, that they did not know that what they were doing could be so devastating.

In this book, I argue otherwise. *Shaking a baby to death is no acci-*

dent any more than burning a child repeatedly with a curling iron, scalding a child in hot water, or slamming a child against a wall until her skull fractures is an accident. All are acts of deliberate harm against human beings who are too young to defend themselves. That's what happened to Christopher.

To anyone outside of his family, Christopher is no more important than any other child who has been killed by a parent or caretaker. I have written about this child because I was called as a witness to his death, and now he has become a particular, special child to me. By telling Christopher's story, I testify to the importance of his life, a testimony that reaches out to all the silenced children whose stories will never be heard.

Ruth Attig, Christopher's grandmother, even while willing to hope that my telling of Christopher will make a difference, is haunted by the despair that she failed him because she didn't speak well enough in the courtroom. "I wasn't good enough, I didn't tell it right," she says. "Really, I don't feel I was given the opportunity—I couldn't say the things I wanted to." She means two things. Literally, there were things she was prohibited from saying by the pretrial motions. The story was not fully told. And then it was not fully heard. For she also means that if only she'd had the right words, she could have gotten the jury to hear the story with her heart and deliver a truly just legal outcome. Telling a story, after all, is only part of the process. The other part is up to the audience. It's the telling *and* the hearing that make stories powerful. Until we are ready to hear and to see, nothing changes.

My position on SBS and my follow-up discussion of child abuse laws and child abuse prevention activities (chapter 9) represent my effort to bring something constructive from this senseless death. I write from an impulse that I share with many people. From the midst of such a meaningless act of violence, we search for some offering of hope, no matter how fragile the possibility. We do not want to dwell on the still, broken body of the child; we want to know there is healing even from this suffering. There is a price exacted for that hope, however, and the price is that we must not look away from what happened to Christopher. If we are to change the ending of this story for others, first, we must own it.

1

Ruth

I bought a white poinsettia for Christopher to place with all the red poinsettias at church last Christmas because in real life he just shone above everyone else.

Wearing a dark shirtwaist dress with a fine print and a lace collar, Ruth Attig walked slowly and carefully to the witness stand, as if moving underwater. Then age fifty-one, she was a youthful grandmother, with her brown, gray-streaked hair pulled back from her face in a short ponytail and tied with a cloth bow.

"Christopher was so curious, and I know you will think it is just a grandmother," she said, turning to the jury, "but he was smart as a tack." For a moment, under that flat, cold courtroom light, her face was warm with memory, and she broke my heart. Her voice was unforgettable.

Her testimony included a showing of the last videotape of Christopher she had made days before he'd been killed. This was Ruth's ninth tape of Christopher, an unselfconscious home movie of the nineteen-month-old sharing a sandwich with Charlie, his "Paw Paw," who drops an affectionate hand on Christopher's head as he stands opening his mouth like a little bird for another bite; climbing and sliding on a dirt pile; trying on a hat and puzzling over a sticker on the front; and at the bidding of Ruth off camera, kissing the boy in the mirror and then turning to grin at her each time.

Ruth is rarely in the Christopher tapes because she's usually the one filming, and she avoids talking on camera because she gets teased about her voice being funny.

"Why?" I asked in the first interview.

"I don't know, they just do," she said.

"Well, tell them to piss off," I replied, and then blanched at my language. I was talking to a church-going Baptist, and I didn't know her well enough to cut loose like that.

"I don't like to talk that bad to people," she demurred.

"I'm sorry," I apologized. But then she continued.

"Today though I did. I've never put anything like this in a letter to someone before in my life." She was writing a letter to a collection agency that was trying to extract payment for Christopher's helicopter bill to St. Louis. The first line said: "You can go to hell."

Having heard her in court, I wasn't surprised at what her voice could carry—a sweet, gentle, almost childlike voice, a voice of tears threaded by steel, trying to fit her love for Christopher into the questions put by prosecution and defense, meeting every question head-on. Freezing a final frame of video where Christopher had been playing outside on a dirt pile, defense lawyer Paul Christenson focused on a spot on Christopher's left temple.

"Do you know what that mark is from?" queried Christenson. He was trying to suggest that Christopher's injuries were attributable to an unspecified accident at Ruth's house, or the result of a fall several weeks earlier.

"It is probably dirt from the dirt pile," she responded.

Christenson wasn't satisfied with this and returned a moment later to the same question.

"Would you agree with me that he does have a mark near the hairline on the left side of his head?"

"Yes," agreed Ruth. And then she snapped back, "Is it on the other pictures of him?"

When Judge David Watt intervened, suggesting that it wasn't up to her to ask the questions, she ducked her head and apologized, embarrassed at the public reproof. At the sentencing hearing, after reading her victim impact statement, she raised her hand to get Judge Watt's attention, asking to speak beyond her written text. She laughed ruefully about that later, raising her hand like a little kid, she said. But her seeming hesitance in the face of authority doesn't prevent her from speaking out when she deems it necessary, even as she frets about the consequences of her brashness. She is not always sure of her power, but she is always sure of her love, and both things—her certainty and her uncertainty—make her a formidable opponent.

As I arrived at Ruth's house for our initial interview, Charlie was removing the remains of an old elm tree, and the smell of cut wood and shavings freshened the warm falling light. Ruth came out and sat on the front steps of her house, and she began talking about Christopher immediately. I sat still, transfixed like a moth by the sad light of her voice as she shone Christopher into the humming twilight. She told me about how Christopher loved her marigolds—once she finally convinced him not to pick them all, he'd carefully put his hands behind his back and squat down to sniff each individual flower, as if the fragrance were unique with each blossom—and how Katie, the Irish setter, curled up on his grave and refused to move the first time they took her to the cemetery.

The interior of her small, ranch-style house is filled with Christopher; his lost life presses from every direction. Here are the sheer, ruffly curtains at the bay window where he played hide-and-seek, here is the chocolate milk stain on the carpet from the night he threw up, and here is the couch where he sometimes napped with Ruth or Charlie or Uncle Tim. Ruth will not change any of these things. There are pictures and mementos of Christopher on the walls, table tops, bay window ledge, china cabinet, and TV. Around the corner in the kitchen, the table is usually covered with Ruth's files and clippings and notes. She is calling prisons to keep track of Gary Gould. She is responding to victims' rights organizations. She is collecting stories about children like Christopher. In the back bedroom that was once his, everything remains as it was when he was last there — except for the boxes of grave decorations Ruth has prepared for him. Slowly, the boxes are taking over the floor space, there are so many of them.

Sorrow has become a palpable quantity in this household. It creeps along the walls, almost a smell. It seeps along the floorboards, almost a sound. It whispers in the opening and closing of doors, almost the voice of the lost child, who will surely come toddling up the hallway any minute to pounce upon the basket of toys so inert beside the hall entranceway, who will scatter his muddy shoes still sitting by the doorway, who will belly laugh when Maw Maw swings him into her arms and plants a thousand kisses in the folds of his neck.

But he is dead, and so is she. I can never know the "old" Ruth Attig, for whoever that plump grandmother was, she is gone, an idealized remnant of past happiness only now fully comprehended in its loss, driven to obsolescence by grief and public scrutiny. When I asked Jackson County State's Attorney Michael Wepsiec if he thought Ruth Attig would want to talk to me about Christopher, he said yes, but he warned me, "She's really a basket case." Wepsiec is a conscientious and thoughtful man, and he worked hard to convict Gary Gould of first degree murder. But he wasn't prepared to deal with the intensity of grieving that is unleashed by the murder of a child. Ruth periodically worried that I would think she was crazy, for some well-meaning friend is always trying to tell her she "needs to get control of her anger," or she "needs to move on and put the past behind her." I was not surprised by her grieving, although I found there was much I didn't understand.

In her victim impact statement, Ruth describes feeling humiliated and shamed by what has happened. Even a year later, she shops mostly at night, traveling the six miles to Carbondale so she won't meet people she knows in Murphysboro. I don't want to look at anyone, she said. I was surprised at her feelings of shame. After all, she hadn't done anything wrong. But from her point of view, this is not true. She failed to protect Christopher, and even though, rationally speaking, she knows there was nothing more she could have done, she blames herself and feels others will too. But just as importantly, it is not only censure she fears, but pity and sympathy as well, for the latter can catch her off guard and find her weeping yet again in the middle of selecting a jar of pickles or purchasing a gallon of milk, exposing her heart once more in the linoleum light of a public place.

The day she testified for Christopher, Ruth remembers being taken out of the courtroom for a break. "I wasn't allowed to talk to anyone, and when they took me out, I had to go to the bathroom, and I was in there just literally screaming and crying my heart out, and [someone] knocked on the door and said I had to come out because the jury wanted in, so I couldn't even cry. And they just sent me over in a corner where everybody could stare at me."

That feeling of being completely exposed, without shelter and comfort, is the constant partner to her grief. I gained a better understanding of what this was like for her one day during a summer trip to the courthouse.

Ruth and I had gone to the courthouse together to read the case file. Because she had been a witness to many of the events recorded, she was going to read the case file to me while I took notes on my laptop. We stopped by Sarah Hinde's office, the court transcriber for the trial, before checking out our files and heading upstairs. Ruth had brought a container of lemon bars for the prosecutor's office. As we were waiting for Sarah, Judge Watt strolled into the room, his after-lunch coffee mug in his hand. The faint look of a man ambushed crossed his face, but he recovered quickly.

"How are you doing, Ruth?" he asked.

"Not so good, Judge Watt," she blurted out, and began crying. Now

Ruth cries a lot when she's with me, so I wasn't surprised at her tears, but I was surprised at the swiftness of her response. She'd been fine a moment ago.

"You've got to give it time, Ruth," he said.

"Here," she sobbed, and bent down to uncover the lemon bars. "You could have a lemon bar with your coffee," and trembling with her weeping, raised her offering to him. "I just made them this morning."

"No, thank you," he said. "I just had lunch, and I've got to get to court in half a minute."

She put the cookies down and turned to him, came close, put her hand on his chest, and looking intently up into his eyes, spoke of Christopher. It was a peculiarly intimate pose, as she tried to explain in the yellow-smelling courthouse, in the fleeting space of the chance encounter, all the pain unanswered by the justice system he represented. Here is why she feels humiliated by Christopher's death. Watt, along with a courtroom of strangers and her entire hometown, has been a voyeur to the inmost regions of her heart. It's an intimacy she did not ask for, and to Watt's credit, he did not shrink from the gesture that affirmed it. But he also had nothing to offer her but commonplaces—what else could he do?—and exited as soon as was decently possible.

After the verdict came in, Ruth went to Christopher's grave to kill herself. She didn't, for now. As I pointed out to her, I couldn't write this book if she didn't at least live long enough to tell me her story. She'd already thought of that, and if there's one thing she wants beyond justice, it's for Christopher's life—as part of her family—to be remembered.

The center of Ruth's life is her family. Her dream was to have a two-story house with a baby in every room, and one thing that attracted her to Charlie Attig was that he was so good with children, always helping them with things and taking time to play and do projects. He was her high school sweetheart, and they married in 1962. Charlie, born and raised in Murphysboro, worked for DX Gas Company and then the Luster Corporation, which later became the Curwood Corporation, where he still works as a printer pressman. His employment was interrupted only by his tour of duty in Vietnam. One of the first married men in Jackson County to be drafted, he returned from Vietnam in 1969.

Two years later, they adopted Chuck. Ruth was twenty-seven, and Chuck was eleven and a half months old. She was twenty-nine when Timmy was born. But "both my boys were first, because Timmy was an infant, but Chuck was our first experience. With Chuck I went from carrying a pencil and notebook to carrying a thirty-pound baby. I would put him in bed and then rub BenGay on my elbows and shoulders, but it was great." When Timmy came along, "my friend told me all that I missed out on was so many thousand diapers, but that wasn't right. I had almost a whole year of stuff to learn about.

"I prayed for my children, and God answered my prayers. And I would thank God every day for Chuck's biological parents. Because I don't know if the father had tried to be a father to him or if he was just a person that planted a seed and went on his way. But as a result of their union, they gave us a beautiful present to care for, and I thank them in their lives for giving us our son. I don't think anyone could love a child any more deeply than I did my two. They were special." For many years now, the Attigs have lived next door to Charlie's parents, side by side with the house where Charlie was raised.

Ruth describes her own childhood as austere, but not without happiness. One of three children, she's a southern Illinois native who attended a one-room schoolhouse near Vergennes. Like a lot of rural children, her pleasures were found in the fields and animals near her house—petting the horse in the pasture next to the house; walking to school in the snow. Her mother used to raise cocker spaniels, and she remembers how much she enjoyed sneaking the puppies into bed with her at night. She knows this sounds corny, but still she says it: "We didn't have a lot of things, but it was a good way to live."

Her stepfather was a construction worker whose seasonal employment often took him away from home. After the family moved into town, her mother was gone a lot as well, managing a local grocery store and later working in a jacket factory to help support the family. These memories spurred her to quit her job before Tim was born in order to spend more time at home with her boys. She got her houseful of children by taking in other children to supplement the family income.

One of Ruth's definitions of "family" is that families spend time together. "As a child growing up I didn't do family things. We went on one family picnic a year, and that was it. I wanted my children to do all of the family things that I felt a family should do, but because of the way my stepdad worked and his drinking problem, we didn't." She and Charlie filled weekends and summers with camping trips and stomper car races and, later, BMX bike racing and neighborhood picnics. Tim says, "There was always a lot of love in the house, and I always knew right from wrong."

Even when there were bike races on Sundays, the Attigs arranged to attend church, either going the night before or attending Sunday school before driving to Sikeston for the day. "I promised God that if he gave us a baby, we'd raise it so he can be proud of it," says Ruth, and she did her best to honor her part of the agreement. Both boys were responsive to their religious upbringing, and Ruth remembers Chuck glumly attributing a racing loss to the fact that he had missed church that day. "We used to think that Chuck was going to grow up to be a preacher because when we'd say prayers, you'd better not even have the food out of the oven yet. If you had it on your plate you're going to eat it cold because when Chuck got started saying his prayers he just kept going. He knew to bring in every little thing that was of importance to him . . . [and] take it to God."

Tim Attig seems to have flourished in this environment, for he successfully negotiated the rapids of adolescence and created a stable adult life for himself. He has an associate's degree in applied science and works in the engineering department at Spartan Light Metal Products. He's taking advantage of a company scholarship plan to further his training by attending courses at Southern Illinois University.

Chuck, however, took a different path. As he grew into adolescence and the teen years, he became increasingly restive; finally his rebelliousness extended to periodic minor scrapes with the law. "I don't know what happened with Chuck," says Tim. "He's the nicest guy I've ever met. But he's just a rough-hewn, or somethin', ya know? It seems like he was a lot more outgoing and daring than [his high school buddies], and they just kind of got boring to him." Ruth remembers struggling to preserve curfew and other house rules in the face of peer pressure, and sometimes she wonders if she was too diligent in trying to keep Chuck on the straight path.

"I don't think she took a lot of shit, you know, from the boys," observed Debbie Phelps, Chuck's companion, who describes Ruth as sweet, unpretentious, and headstrong. "She's worked hard to keep her family together. They've had a lot of problems with Chuck since he was fourteen or fifteen years old, and they'd kind of hardened themselves to him. Almost in a way given up on him . . . still loving him but not wanting to put their hand out because they've been stepped on so many times by him. And they were."

Looking back, Ruth is not sure what can be used to explain Chuck's increasingly crooked path. "I guess in one way we gave him too many things. [Charlie] has said that he wanted his children to have all the things that he always wanted but never did get to have, so our boys had the best bicycles, they had motorcycles at an early age." But, as Ruth says, there comes a time when parents don't have enough money to keep buying everything a child wants. They tried to impress upon the boys the necessity of saving and planning ahead. Each boy had a savings account, and periodically, they were allowed to spend the interest.

As they got older and their desires became more complicated, they would borrow money from Ruth to purchase that new three-wheeler or motorcycle. Tim always paid his money back, but Ruth learned to make Chuck sign a note with her because it was the only way she had a chance of getting her money back. Even that didn't always work, which is how Ruth ended up owning Chuck's three-wheeler.

After Chuck graduated from high school, he moved in and out of the house several times. Finally, he wanted to move back home. Ruth and Charlie talked it over and agreed, but stipulated that he would have to abide by house rules and pay $30 a month rent to help cover basic expenses. Chuck was outraged. This was his home, and he shouldn't have to pay for staying there! Indignantly, he moved elsewhere. Then, he met Rhonda Carter.

Ruth is angry with Chuck. Through his impulsive, careless ways, he has brought to her life the unending pain of Christopher's loss. More-over, Chuck is impatient with the drama of her grief; they can't even agree on whether or how to have a memorial service to mark the one-year anniversary of Christopher's death. But Ruth doesn't deliver Chuck to me, although she easily could, for her anger is a complicated rope of love and loathing.

Unlike Gary Gould, Chuck only has misdemeanors on his record, she tells me very early in our relationship. Either she is deliberately misleading me, or she doesn't know the extent of his record. I am afraid to ask her which is the case, for either way, such a question will violate a carefully constructed shelter. "What lengths would you go to for your children?" she asks. "He's been hurt enough during the past two and a half years. I have hated him in the past — maybe not him so much as his way of living and his actions. But I . . . could not live with myself if I did or said something that would upset Chuck and send him over the edge." Moreover, while he's been hard on her, she feels she can't blame him, for in her grief, she has failed to be there for him as she should have been. A death like this does not bring a family closer together, not even a family that once prayed together and camped together and cheered at the races.

Ruth is embarrassed to cry as she does, and she knows it is so easy to dismiss her because of it. That may be one reason why she's agreed to talk with me about Christopher. She thinks I can give voice to what she can't. So, she is afraid of driving me away. And then again, she is simply afraid. My listening and recording will be one more public exposure, and she cannot control what I will think of her life, any more than she could control what the jury did with the verdict.

I am afraid of disappointing her.

One afternoon in July, I came over to her house to watch some videos of Christopher. I had concluded the formal interviewing, but we always talked a lot on these visits, and I learned to reserve most of the afternoon when I was going to "see" Christopher. Ruth had been explaining the video scenes I was watching, and she seemed to be in a calm mood. But, as was often the case, Ruth became most intense just as I was preparing to leave.

"There's something I want you to understand," she said. I was gathering my notebook and papers and shaking out my stiff legs. "I wish I could tell you, make you see, how precious he was." She paused, and then as tears filled her eyes, she said, "I should have saved him, and I didn't. I knew he was being hurt, and I didn't report it because I was afraid Rhonda would never let me see him again. But I should have reported it, and I said that to Mr. Wepsiec, and he said he'd have to prosecute me, too. And I said that would be fine. I want to be prosecuted for murder. They should have prosecuted me, too."

"Ruth," I said, halted in my tracks like a worm just smartly pecked by a large bird, "you did the best you could. You couldn't have saved him." Uneasily, I began shuffling through my belongings, now piled haphazardly in my arms in my arrested exit. Her intensity, never alarming to me before, had taken a new tone.

"You've always had good instincts about Christopher's well-being, and I know you did the best you could."

"Well, you must be the only person who thinks so. And you must think I'm going crazy. That I am crazy."

"No, not at all. I've never thought that about you." This was absolutely true, but how could I show her? Awkwardly, I reached around my armload of stuff to pat her on the arm.

She looked away from me and, her fingers twisting helplessly against one another, gasped through her tears, "But you're educated, so you could be hiding what you really think from me." Her words were accusatory, but her tone was pleading. The enormity of what I had promised to do prickled down my skin like a cold rain.

We stood facing each other, pictures of the dead child flickering behind us on the television screen. Christopher in the neonatal unit at Carbondale Memorial, his body so tiny that Ruth's hand nearly covers it entirely; Chuck struggling to dress the rubbery little preemie; Rhonda, huge circles under her eyes, giving him his first bottle. Later, the flourishing child, rubbing noses with Paw Paw; roughhousing with Tim and riding on Katie; chopping up the dog food with his new tomahawk. I had been watching something I could never understand. I know what a nineteen-month-old child is like, but I had never known this particular nineteen-month-old child, the only one named Christopher Michael Attig who was loved by Ruth and who is irreplaceably gone. I wanted so much to give her something comforting, something useful. Now, I saw how foolish I'd been.

Ruth was hopelessly marooned far away from me, and I didn't put down my books to hug her. There was no gesture, there was no word. I couldn't move. I just began to cry with her.

"I guess you don't trust me," I finally said, snuffling. "I guess I'm going to have to work harder on that."

She looked at me wordlessly, eyes spilling.

"I'm so afraid I'm forgetting Christopher," she said. "I've been testing myself to see if I can remember things about him that aren't on the video. He loved feeding the squirrels at my mother's house, mostly because he got to eat more peanuts than he gave to the squirrels. I can see him, leaning over his stroller and babbling and pointing at the squirrels, and trying to stuff unshelled nuts into his mouth. It was hard to convince him to take the shells off first. But I'm afraid I'm losing my memories, and I'll only have the videos, and someday they'll wear out. And I'll forget him. My memory hasn't been good since the stroke, anyway; except for Christopher, I remember everything."

"You will remember what I need to understand. Please," I continued, "just keep talking to me, no matter how awful it seems. I don't think you're crazy, and I never will."

Until this day, I'd never known if Ruth could hear me when I talked, and our conversations outside the interviews had been virtually nonexistent. All of our contacts were defined by the crisis and urgency of Christopher's death, as if it had just happened yesterday—because for Ruth, that's exactly how it feels. But something turned that day we cried together, standing before the moving pictures of what she'd lost. We began talking more on the phone, trading legal and personal news relative to the case and others like it. She gave me a pretty, soft book for my children, and I showed her pictures. I went with her to a meeting of St. Louis Parents of Murdered Children, and we talked all the way there and all the way back. Then we went to the courthouse again to finish reading the case file.

It was late in the afternoon and we were working our way through the bond revocation hearing. After fatally assaulting Christopher on August 3, 1994, Gould had been charged in October and had been out on $5,000 bail since November. Then, on December 24, 1994, he allegedly committed aggravated criminal sexual assault and harassment of a witness. To be specific, he allegedly held a knife to Rhonda Carter's throat and raped her. The state, accordingly, moved to revoke his bond. Ruth was reading and summarizing Rhonda's testimony in the matter.

Rhonda was getting ready for work, and expecting to meet Chuck to go to the cemetery and visit Christopher's grave. Hearing boot steps outside the trailer where she was staying, Rhonda thought it was Chuck, but when she opened the door, it was Gary, who pushed his way in. He grabbed her, pulled out a knife, held it to her eye and her throat and said . . . Here Ruth paused, looked at me appraisingly, and then read in a deliberate voice, *"I'll slice your fuckin' throat, bitch."* She was careful to leave the "g" off of "fuckin'."

"The feds are all over my ass," Ruth continued reading, stopping to explain that "feds" is local tough-guy terminology for police.

Then he got up. "He was pacing back and forth," says Rhonda. "I was crying. He changed his whole attitude. He went from being real mad. He was like, wiping tears off my face, telling me that he loved me and, oh, God, that he missed me and all this crap."

I looked at Ruth. Her voice had taken on a suspiciously theatrical tone. But she kept on reading and summarizing.

Rhonda told him that things weren't like they used to be, which apparently made him decide to prove otherwise, because that's when he raped her—Ruth paused a moment to calculate—*about a two-minute intercourse. Then he tells her to get up and admire his new car.*

"We could go anywhere in the U.S. in that car," he says. "We could sell it and get something different, and it could be just like it used to be."

"You're making that up," I accused, as Ruth paused. It seemed like bad dialogue from a B-movie villain.

"No," she said. "I wish I was."

"Is that all?" I asked hopefully. It felt bad to be plowing so methodically through Rhonda's testimony.

"Nope. He asks her if he can come back again."

"I don't care what you do," replies Rhonda. So he leans over and kisses her on the forehead and says, "I love you, baby."

Ruth intoned "baby" in a deep, slouchy voice. I stopped typing, and she stopped reading for a moment.

"There's more," she said. "Here's Christenson on the cross-examination. He accuses Rhonda of being an incredible witness who is just out to discredit his client, and he is arguing that there is no evidence of real force: 'There is no evidence there was an assault. The testimony was that at the time of the sex there was no knife to the throat. That was the testimony, Your Honor.' Then Watt answers: 'My experience has been in most sexual assaults that the individual who is doing the assaulting does not have a knife at the throat; they're using their hands for other things.'"

Something about the way this sounds as she reads it startles us both. It sounds funny, and for a moment we crimp our lips and look down, letting the incongruity and pathos of the exchange wash past us, willing the tension of the long afternoon to take shape as a suitable expression. Then, with relief, we forge ahead to what we know is the outcome of the hearing. The court finds Rhonda convincing (though, for various reasons, the state did not file charges against Gould for the sexual assault), revokes Gary's bail, and puts him back in jail to await trial for Christopher's murder.

That day, I got one more glimpse of the tart, wicked sense of humor owned by the Ruth who precedes all her really harsh remarks with "God forgive me for saying this, but . . ." "Did you hear Christenson?" she asked me as we exchanged phone confidences about the sentencing hearing. "He must have used the word 'superfluous' three times in ten minutes. Must have been on his word-of-the-month calendar." In a similar way, she described to me how Gary once nearly ran her down in the trailer driveway: "He came tearing in there, and came right up to me. I was holding Christopher, and I jumped back because I thought he was going to hit me. Then he turned onto the grass in front of the trailer, wheels throwing rocks every which way, and stopped. He jumped out of the truck and raced into the trailer. Maybe he had diarrhea, or had to answer the phone, or needed to jump into bed with someone."

I'd suspected that the "old" Ruth could be a pithy commentator when provoked, but I'll grant what Ruth would say about the matter: this is the new Ruth, the not-very-nice, paranoid, distrustful Ruth. This is the new Ruth writing "You can go to hell" or calmly reading "I'll slice your fuckin' throat, bitch" in that sweet, childlike voice. This is the new Ruth, whose voice will never, ever stop talking for Christopher.

2

Joyce

I would ask him for a kiss and he wouldn't give me a kiss for nothing. But I would say, "No, you're not going to kiss me," and he would shower me with kisses. So I would say, "Don't you kiss me, no, no, no," and I would act like I couldn't stand it. And he would kiss me all over.

L ike heat lightning flickering at the margins of a sullen twilight, the troubled relationship between the two halves of Christopher's family barely made a glimmer in the courtroom. Pretrial motions and the exclusion of collateral issues prevented the defense from refocusing attention upon Rhonda, although Christenson tried to do so in his cross-examination of Ruth.

Q: Now Mrs. Attig, you loved this little boy very much, isn't that true?

A: That's very true.

Q: And isn't it also true that you considered trying to get custody of Christopher?

Mr. Wepsiec: Objection.

The Court: Sustained.

Q: Is it true, Mrs. Attig, that you suspected Rhonda Carter of physical abuse?

Mr. Wepsiec: Objection.

The Court: Sustained.

This exchange is one of the few places where an interfamily conflict is hinted at. Because the prosecution successfully kept attention focused on Gould, there was little said in court that revealed much about the Attig and Carter/Lockhart family relationships.

I didn't have any idea who Joyce Lockhart was until the sentencing hearing. She'd been subpoenaed by the defense, and as a result had been barred from the courtroom. But she was never called to testify, and she was barely mentioned in the trial. Later, Joyce said that she thought Christenson had subpoenaed her just to keep her out of the courtroom during the trial. Gary might be intimidated by her. I could see why. Where Ruth's anger flooded her eyes, Joyce's anger was a dry, scornful heat. She could have withered green grass with the glare she turned upon Gary Gould at the sentencing hearing.

I never became close to Joyce as I did with Ruth, for while she was always cordial when we talked, Joyce also maintained her distance. She wanted to believe I would do her no harm, but she'd seen too much in her life to trust that belief. And she was right. I could not promise her that I would tell her story in a way that would vindicate her family. Our first conversation was typical of both her vulnerability and her insight into human relationships. When I called her to see if she and her family wanted to talk about Christopher, she was cautious with me. She immediately made sure I knew I'd be hearing a different perspective on Gary Gould. "We don't hate him in this household; our feelings about it are ambivalent," she explained.

"That's okay," I replied. "The idea is to tell Christopher's story and give his family a chance to speak. You don't have to see everything the same way as Ruth Attig does, and no one should feel like they are on trial."

"Well, I'm sure you're hearing a lot from that side," she said. Then I asked her about a meeting time, and still she hesitated.

"What is it?" I asked. To my dismay, she began crying. "I'm afraid you've already prejudged us all," she stated flatly.

As I came to realize, my presence as a listener moving back and forth between the two households put them at risk of a greater vulnerability before each other, one that neither household could well tolerate. I was in danger of hearing too much and possibly tracking hurtful story fragments where they didn't belong. So, it was an arduous mental journey back and forth between households, and even the location of each family seemed to lend credence to an ongoing sense of psychological tension. The Attig family lives on one edge of Murphysboro, the house on a dead-end street that marks a natural, geographic margin. Immediately south, the neighborhood banks downward. At the bottom of the slope is a series of small houses that trail toward the city limits. Joyce Lockhart lives with her husband, Kevin Lockhart, her daughters, Rhonda and Robyn Carter, from her first marriage, and her fourteen-year-old son with Kevin, Wayne Lee, whom everyone calls Buddy. They are right up against the city limits, on the opposite side of Murphysboro from the Attig family.

The house Joyce lives in has always belonged to the Lockhart family. The original face of the house slips up from beneath the imposed modernity of improvements — an upper-story addition, central air conditioning, and new window shutters — giving the building a curious blurred look as though it might always be moving imperceptibly. But the paint is peeling in places and the stone lions guarding the porch steps have lost so much ear and tail they might well be fierce lambs, ready to pounce upon enemies. Several scraggly potted plants sit by the front door, as if waiting to be let in after a long, tiring night of revelry.

Six generations of Lockharts have occupied this hundred-year-old dwelling, and yet despite the fixity of that fact, Joyce herself has moved at least five times in the last sixteen years, from Murphysboro to California, then back to the Illinois towns of Gorham and Cahokia, finally returning to Murphysboro. She has been married to Kevin Lockhart all that time, but the ancestral house has been home for only six of those married years. I commented to Kevin that Joyce seemed an unlikely person to get confined to the family homestead.

"Oh yeah, oh God, she is a gypsy," said Kevin, "there's no doubt about that. She likes to go." In fact, he, too, is no stranger to mobility. Although he was raised in the house he now lives in, he recalls a childhood marked by frequent moves from Detroit to West Virginia until his parents finally settled upon a Murphysboro business and brought the Lockhart name back to the family house.

Kevin enjoys fixing and rebuilding things and in times past has worked as a free-lance contractor and an auto mechanic. Despite his thirty-eight years, with his wavy red-gold hair brushing his collar, he could easily pass for much younger. The warmth of flesh under his chin could be the embrace of middle age, or it could just be baby fat. Behind the house are his vehicles — a boat and trailer, an RV, a pickup truck and several cars in various states of mechanical undress. They are parked, beached, abandoned, waiting, metal bodies picked clean and grounded by a tumultuous family life. In Joyce's family, someone is always just about to get on with it, turn a corner, start a new life. They are constantly on the move from jobs, houses, and sometimes relationships, and the big old house is open to others who are similarly mobile — friends or relations passing through, fleeing bad environments, crashing for unspecified reasons. The interior of the house has the dark, waiting feel of a refuge. The living room curtains are always drawn, and the dense line of giant holly bushes that bristle across the front and around the wrap porch protects the occupants against any accidental invasion of light or prying eyes. The house is cool and clean, despite the flurries of family life that spill through its hallways.

Rhonda has always been susceptible to waifs and orphans, both Joyce and Robyn said. "If there is someone who doesn't have friends, someone who has low self-esteem, someone who needs a place to stay, Rhonda was going to drag these kids home. She's been doing it all her life. She gets 'I feel sorry for someone' and 'I love someone' mixed up.

And I think it's often misconstrued that Rhonda is this wild woman, and I think really it's just she wants to help people do better and doesn't know how and goes about it the wrong way," Joyce explains.

Rhonda is a young twenty-three-year-old with many faces. In the courtroom she was carefully made-up, her face controlled and grave. She sat straight, her hands tightly entwined in her lap. When she was irritated at the defense lawyer, she would widen her eyes and jerk her chin slightly, a trace of teenage insolence in the face of the proceedings.

> Q: Now isn't it true that you told the police that you were using drugs on Tuesday?
>
> A: No, sir. I said I may have used drugs, I don't recall.
>
> Q: You don't know whether you were or not?
>
> A: I may have smoked a joint in that time.
>
> Q: During the time Gary was gone?
>
> A: I may have, yes. [Eyes wide, there is that pouty shake of her head and just a whisper of defiance in her tone: a two-second moue that says, "You can't make me say more, can you Mr. Lawyer Man?"]

But under other circumstances, in her family portrait mode — full mouth, polished cheekbones, and fashionably teased bangs — she is simply an attractive young woman in a series of arranged faces. And then, there is a photo of Rhonda and Chuck taken before they got married. Chuck is an immense man, well over six feet tall, and Rhonda, who is at least five and a half feet, looks like a doll perched on his lap. She is slim, dressed in a party dress with a short, sassy black skirt. Despite the artful tumble of her dark hair, her smiling face looks no more than twelve or thirteen years old.

Next to her impetuous older sister, nineteen-year-old Robyn is the taken-for-granted, responsible child. Yet Robyn doesn't want to get married and have children, at least not right away. She's seen what's happened to her contemporaries, if not her own sister—young women rushing into marriage only to find themselves trapped with an infant, a free-range husband, and miles between themselves and the next good time. "Mom always told me, you know, you don't have to grow up when you're nineteen years old, you can still be a kid until you're twenty-five. And you might as well have your young life while you got it because you're never going to get it again. I'm not going to ruin my young life for marriage; it's not worth it."

Ironically enough, Robyn alternated with Joyce as the designated adult in the family. She took care of Christopher when Rhonda could or would not. At that time, she was working forty hours a week managing a local movie theater and going to college. What was Rhonda doing? "She was living her young life, that's what she was doing," says Robyn with a smile.

While Ruth's living room has become a shrine to Christopher, Joyce's house has been washed clean by grieving and circumstance, leaving only a few pictures behind. Christopher broke their camcorder so they don't have a tape library like Ruth does. And many of Rhonda's pictures were held hostage by Gary. When he threw her out of the trailer, he gave her ten minutes to collect all of her possessions. She fled with mostly clothing, leaving personal mementos behind. Joyce believes that the undeveloped rolls of film and pictures have all been destroyed.

No matter. Joyce is an articulate storyteller, and she speaks in vivid images and with a spirited sense of narrative drama. Although she worries that people will think she didn't love Christopher because her grieving is not displayed like Ruth's, it is clear that her important pictures are carried in her mind's eye, close to her heart. Her household has absorbed and integrated his loss, which is a form of grief management that would be typical of Joyce. She's a defiant survivor of hard times, and she's learned to stand back up, no matter how bitter the blow, and keep on going.

Joyce is a youthful grandmother at age forty, a plump, pretty woman
with a square jaw, wide, full mouth, and sparkling green eyes. Her
youthfulness may be as willed as her optimism, both poignant responses to her own troubled childhood.

"I'm the oldest of five kids. I have a dad who is an alcoholic. My dad
beat on my mom horribly, I mean horribly. It was not an uncommon
thing for Dad to beat her to the point that she had to be hospitalized.
My dad beat on my brother, to the point that I have dragged my brother
to the neighbors and begged them to call the police, and of course the
police did nothing." In those days, the police didn't intervene in family disputes, and it fell to Joyce to mediate family explosions. She became a surrogate parent in her family, trying to keep peace so her dad
didn't get angry.

"My mom was a hard worker, but she didn't always take care of her
house. Mom was the kind [who'd say] 'Let's go on a picnic' seven days
a week. And sometimes it's fun but it's kind of like she never grew up."

Absent a mother who could protect her, Joyce was not only physically abused but also sexually abused. Her most vivid and painful
memories are of her sexual vulnerability as she neared adolescence
and young womanhood. Edgar, a man who seemed to hang about the
house, was in the habit of initiating "manipulation and sexual play"
with her. But one afternoon he trapped twelve-year-old Joyce in the
barn, and she knew the games were over. She had the gumption to start
screaming until a neighbor came with a shotgun, ran Edgar off, and
waited with her until her dad came home. His response? He was angry
at Joyce for involving a neighbor. The constant message of her childhood was that she wasn't worth anything.

"I'm not a person that sits around with a low self-esteem or feels I
don't have self-worth. I do. But I think those feelings [of self-esteem]
came from my own, that I struggled for myself to find that," she says,
acutely aware of the emotional deprivations that have marked her own
development.

Her immediate solution to her situation was to get married. She did
so at age seventeen, right after her father tried to kill her. "When I was
sixteen, I wrecked my father's truck. I took it on a road I shouldn't have
been on, and when I came home, my father went to work, but I knew
he was very angry." Joyce waited anxiously at home that evening, unsure which was more dangerous, staying or running. She was standing
in front of the picture window, uneasily peering out into the darkness,
when she heard her father return. It was eleven o'clock at night. A minute later, the window glass shattered around her as her father pulled
out his .38 and took aim at her. Screaming, she dived for the floor as
her brother ran for the shotgun. Her father aimed several more shots at
the house. "Just send her out, and everybody will be okay," he bellowed. But her brother held him off until the police arrived and arrested him. "He probably would have killed me, he probably would
have beaten me to death," she said. "That's when I decided, 'I'm getting out of this.' It was a matter of me living or not living."

So Joyce married John Carter, whom she did not love, but who loved
her and would take her away from the threatening house of her father.
During the seven-year marriage, they had two daughters, Rhonda and
Robyn, and she went back to school to study accounting. But John was
jealous, fearing she'd meet attractive young men in the accounting
program, so he decided she could stay in school as long as she was working on a nursing degree, presumably because it was a female-saturated
field. Later, he decided he wouldn't pay for her schooling, but with the
help of a Comprehensive Employment Training Act grant and her
mother's support, Joyce got her nursing degree. It gave her both voca-
tional versatility and financial safety. John "was pretty good to me, but
it was hard to live with an alcoholic" who began abusing her "at
the end when he realized that I was going to leave him." She divorced
John, marrying Kevin in 1979. They met while he was a guard and she
was a medical technician at Menard State Prison.

Joyce was only seventeen when she had Rhonda, "so I grew up with her." She thinks maybe she was a harsh parent, but Kevin says otherwise. As she reflects on this, perhaps he isn't too far off the mark. "If my kids want to do something or want something, it's my goal to provide that, whatever it is," she explains. She is always looking for ways to secure "happiness for them."

For Joyce, it is important to be open to her children, even if there are things going on their lives she doesn't approve of. "[M]y children have to be able to come to me and say anything, such as, 'I went to a party and we did cocaine.'" She may not like hearing this, but at least her children are talking with her. "I never ever want to do anything that closes the line of communication," she says. "I have seen that happen in so many families and the kids lie and then the parents suddenly don't know how their kid could be involved in this." Joyce's child-rearing philosophy was really put to the test with Rhonda, because "if anything bad was going to happen, it was going to happen to Rhonda."

Joyce is proud of her daughters, both of whom placed as winners in the American Legion "Voice of Democracy" speech contest. But she seems to be most powerfully identified with Rhonda, whose tragic early marriage has demanded so much family energy as to displace most other claims. Rhonda and Joyce don't always agree or get along; nonetheless, "she's always the one I fall back on in everything," says Rhonda.

Chuck didn't like for Rhonda "to wear makeup or clothes that I had bought her because it showed too much of her body, you know? I figured she has a nice body, why not wear those kind of things, she looked cute in them," Joyce says. Rhonda's tumultuous relationship with Chuck was often conducted with the assistance of her mother, who waded into the fray when she felt her daughter's safety or well-being was at issue. "We fought pretty seriously, we fought a lot," Joyce says, recalling her relationship with Chuck. "I was in the bathtub one time taking a bath and Chuck was threatening Rhonda, so Rhonda comes into the bathroom with me. My daughters have always been in the bathroom when I'm taking a bath, but here comes Chuck. I said,

'No you're not, I'm in the bathtub,' and he just kept on. So my mother, who is a very big woman, grabbed him by the nape of the neck and threw him out."

Her concern for Rhonda is perhaps most visible at those times when she swings a story Rhonda's direction no matter what the starting point, always making sure that her daughter is not forgotten. Joyce confesses to sending a customized card to defense lawyer Paul Christenson on behalf of Christopher that said, "Thanks for nothing. Had I been given the chance to grow up I would have known better than to associate with the likes of you." Then she went to the grave site to tell Christopher what she'd done: "I want you to know that I did that and it was not very nice but Grandma did it for you and I wish I could have punched him [Christenson] in the nose, because he made my daughter sound terrible."

Unfortunately, her protective love for Rhonda coupled with her vigilant hopefulness, no matter how dire the situation, made it difficult for her to respond to Christopher's situation. Both Ruth and Joyce mentioned two injuries to Christopher that might have signaled prior abuse. One was a strange red welt that ran from the back of his neck, around the side crease, and across his chest, something like a rope burn, judging from Ruth's pictures. The other was a mark on Christopher's face, the outline of a hand print, as if someone had whacked the child from behind and above, across his ear and jaw.

When Joyce saw the fading yellow finger bruise lines on Christopher's face, she was horrified. She tried to match her hand to the bruises to gauge the size of hand that had left such a mark. Her hand was too small. She called Kevin to see Christopher's face.

"He's either been grabbed and shaken, or he's been just grabbed, but my God, if you shake a baby you could kill him," she informed Kevin.

When Rhonda came home, Joyce met her at the door.

"I want to know right now what happened to this baby. He isn't my child, but you better tell me what happened. There were never bruises on you like that that someone wasn't asking me, and I want to know," she demanded.

Rhonda was mad at being confronted, but she told Joyce that she'd already talked to Gary, who said that the dog jumped up and got Christopher on the face.

Joyce was skeptical that the dog could have made finger marks, but she didn't know how much to push the issue with her daughter. "Ruth was trying to take Christopher away from Rhonda based on abuse, and there was no abuse." Besides, the pit bull, Bonnie, was "forever jumping on Christopher."

Yet, she remained uncertain. She felt in her heart that Gary was telling a fish tale about the finger marks, but then again, there was the possibility he was telling the truth. She finally decided that Christopher had been abused once or twice, but not on a regular basis, and that the other mark, the funny red welt on his neck, "was probably really [from] the dog because it was all zigzagged."

"Would it be fair to say that your judgment in assessing what was happening to Christopher was clouded by your desire to protect Rhonda?"

"Yes. That's a very fair thing to say."

Joyce protects Rhonda; Ruth protects Chuck. Their puzzled, pained love for their children who've gone wrong is but one thing they have in common, but also the one thing that prevented them from uniting their strengths to protect Christopher. Ruth and Joyce did not know each other before their feckless children got married, but what they came to know of each other did not lead to a warm friendship.

"Ruth and I have always had a real problem with each other," Joyce says candidly, agreeing that it didn't help Rhonda and Chuck's fragile marriage to have the two mothers-in-law so estranged from each other. A good deal of this stemmed from each mother's assessment of the other's child. As Chuck put it, "Joyce thought her daughter could do so much better, which maybe she could have, and then my mother thought that maybe I could have done better." Joyce liked Chuck except when he abused Rhonda; Ruth found that Rhonda's initial charm wore off as she and Chuck carried on dramatic fight/reunion scenes with each other. Later, when Rhonda got custody of Christopher, Ruth was appalled at the way she took care of the child, an outlook vigorously combated by the protective Joyce.

When Joyce delivered her victim impact statement, she read in a firm, clear voice, looking up frequently to glare at Gary. The format was generic, a prepared question/answer sequence, which included a series of questions about financial loss, such as expenses incurred for hospitalization, counseling, or lost wages as a result of the crime in question. Joyce steadfastly refused to name any price, declaring at each point, "Not important." Her refusal of the questions is as typical of her as Ruth's acceptance of the same questions.

"I was real offended by the fact that they wanted to know how much money I spent on anything, and then I got aggravated at Ruth because she knew down to the nickel what she had spent. It's like I never kept track of that part. It had nothing to do with what I wanted to say."

"I wish I were more like her," Ruth says wistfully. "Joyce always speaks right up for herself."

It's not that Ruth, who still burns over Gould getting bail money back, is somehow miserly or grasping. She didn't like the financial questions either, and at the sentencing hearing she extemporized one of her answers, insisting, "You can't put a value on a baby's life." The difference between the two doesn't have to do with money but with their differing perception of boundaries and authority. It would never have occurred to Ruth not to answer the questions. She's something of a literalist about form. Joyce, whose whole life has been marked by boundary transgressions against her, has no such regard for form, so she felt free to ignore what seemed irrelevant to her. Consequently, Ruth *would* look prissy and sanctimonious next to Joyce; Joyce *would* look sloppy and profane next to Ruth. They were never meant to be in such proximity, making each other look bad. "Ruth didn't roughhouse with Christopher, but I did. We boxed, we kicked, we pinched, we aggravated." One day shortly before Christopher was killed, Joyce settled in to take a bath. The bathroom has two entrances, so an enterprising child could gallop through the bathroom and around the front bedrooms and living room in a big circle. Joyce had put up the child gates at the back hallway and let Christopher loose. "I'd lay back in the bathtub and had my eyes shut, and he runs through and pinches me on the breast, and has this little look like he knew he shouldn't have done that, and took off running. And I thought, 'I can't do this any longer. Time for Grandma to take a bath alone.' I mean it was funny, it was embarrassing, and I thought, 'Oh my God, what if the Attigs knew this. I don't want them to think anything weird.'" But nonetheless, she tells me the story, relishing the account of her mischievous grandson.

Says Ruth, "At least when he was with me I knew that he was okay, that he's safe, he's loved, he's fed properly. He's living what I call a decent life at our house, and I'm not saying I'm the greatest because I'm not, I'm far from it, but he had a far better life when with us than he ever had with his mother."

Even the grandmothers' descriptions of Christopher himself, by no means mutually exclusive, can't quite hold hands. For Ruth, Christopher was the beautiful, innocent little boy who always shared his toys and his food. "If you asked Christopher for something, he'd just give it to you and smile." He was her angel. "Christopher was so tender with Courtney at Sunday school. Like he knew she was different and you had to be so careful around her." Some of her fondest moments with him were times of quiet tenderness, sleeping with him on restless nights, loving the warmth of his head nestled on her shoulder as the well-fed baby relaxed for an after-lunch nap. For Joyce, Christopher was the rowdy little boy who was rather jealous of his toys, "not really

the sharing kind, and that was okay, because he was the only one."
Christopher could always make them laugh with his silly, and sometimes naughty, antics. Some of her happiest stories are about his ram-
bunctious physical energy. Certainly Christopher roughhoused in the
Attig household, with his uncle Timmy, for example, as every video
attests, and certainly he spent quiet, peaceful times in the Carter/
Lockhart household, with his young uncle Buddy, for instance, sometimes using the boy as a pillow for napping. Yet Ruth and Joyce's di-
verging portraits of Christopher attest to the simple fact that Christopher led parallel lives in two households.

"This was his home, this was considered his home, and this is where
he thought was home, too," says Joyce firmly, referring to her house.
"He went to Ruth's every Saturday and sometimes in the evenings, but
the majority of time, getting up was in this home, and the majority of
time, going to bed was in this home."

Says Ruth, equally firm, "This was his home, you know, he wasn't
just a visitor, he lived here."

Neither grandmother realized how much the other was keeping the
little boy, or how much they have had in common.

Both Ruth and Joyce have preserved Christopher's room in their
house, and each is still protective of his toys and clothing, reluctant to
let other children handle his things. Each one confesses that she feels
like a bad person because she can't bring herself to disperse his things
to children who could use them, but neither can bear to part with toys
and clothing that still bear his trace and scent. At Ruth's house, the toy
car purchased right after he was returned to Rhonda for the last time
still waits for him on the bed, along with his stuffed toys. There is the
bear with the heart that blinked in time to little songs that comforted
him in the night, and the bear that says "Chiggers" across the front, because Charlie said Christopher was so little and so red, he was "Paw
Paw's little chigger." At Joyce's house there is the giant plastic airplane
with all his "slobbers" still on it because no one can bear to wash it; one

tiny preemie diaper, a sad reminder of his miraculous beginning; his big floppy hat; and the stuffed monkey dressed in a jogging outfit that Christopher once wore. It says "I love Grandma."

"Whenever we have a particularly hard time, any of us, we come in this room and we sit in here and play with his hat, or we hold his toys," says Joyce.

Both Ruth and Joyce have been told their grieving is excessive by tactless acquaintances and friends. Joyce remembers sitting with Christopher's jacket, "bawling, and the jacket is kind of dirty, but it smelled like him. I can't smell him any more, so I can smell the jacket." The whole family thought she was going crazy. "I couldn't hardly make it through Wal-Mart because I'd have to go past the baby department. I had three relatives having baby showers, and it took me three trips to buy gifts. I had to leave the store in tears the first two times." Both women found it difficult even to be around small children in the months immediately following Christopher's death.

Both grandmothers were trying to make a safe place for Christopher. Despite his journey between the two households, not to mention the time he spent with Rhonda and Gary and Chuck and Debbie, no one reported any discernible ill effects for him, although Ruth worried about his stability. "When he opened his little eyes, did he know where he was? I had one way of rocking him and holding him when he would take his bottle, and he'd finger my hair. How does he know that he belongs to all these people? Or, because he started his life like that, does he just accept anybody and everybody?" But Joyce feels that because he was so little when he started his domestic traveling, he was used to it, and "maybe Ruth and I both tried to compensate for Chuck and Rhonda not being together."

Joyce was watching, doing her best to make a shelter for Christopher, because she knows what it is like to be battered and lonely. "I spent my entire life looking for a safe place, and when I became an adult, I wanted to make a safe place for children, and then for Christo-

pher, my first and only grandchild. I wanted him to feel safe here."
When she took him to Gary and Rhonda, "I didn't have a car seat, so I
would put him in the bucket seat next to me, strap him in, and I would
always hold on to his leg. Then I would drive very carefully, and
we would go out to the trailer. And I would go, 'Mommy, Mommy,
Mommy, Mommy,' and he would just laugh and his face would light
up, and when we hit the left curve, I'd go, 'Gary, Gary, Gary, Gary,'
and he would be just as excited. So I'm thinking there must be some
love there from Gary, because if there is not, Christopher wouldn't feel
that way about him."

And yet, both women were suspicious of Gary. Ruth knew she was
in a precarious position, however, and not a terribly objective one, either. As Chuck's mother, she naturally would be hostile to the man
who had replaced her son in Rhonda's affections. She was afraid if she
spoke up about Gary and Rhonda's life-style, Rhonda would refuse to
let her see Christopher. But she never did like Gary, and although she
portrays herself as a discreet observer of a dangerous situation, she ob-
viously managed to communicate her disapproval, because Gary reported that "Ruth has a tendency to interfere with Rhonda and her raising Christopher. Ruth just likes to get involved where she is not really
needed. She will make comments that are not actually true, but that
was the way she is."

But while Ruth tends to see things in absolutes, leaving little room
for ambiguity, Joyce tends to travel back and forth between evidences,
unable to draw a line. She had a "gut instinct" about Gary. There was
something "self-centered" about him that made her uneasy. When "I
came dragging in the carousel horse for Christopher, Gary laughed,
but if you could have seen the look on his face, it was almost like a jeal-
ousy," as if she should have spent the money on him. "And I often got
that picture, but then I would think maybe I'm misreading because I
was really hard about Chuck, so this time I'm trying to keep quiet." She
saw Gary tending to Christopher, changing diapers, or getting up with

him in the night, so evidence of his indifference or even physical abuse was hard to assess. She was watching, but "I thought maybe I'm seeing things wrong." Like Ruth, she was afraid Rhonda would shut her out if she spoke up, and she was mindful that Kevin had already antagonized Rhonda by voicing his negative opinion. And then again, Ruth, who wanted to take custody of Christopher, "was calling and saying real negative things about Gary," which could only be seen as an attack on Rhonda, and Joyce's instincts are always to protect her family. Just like Ruth.

"Ruth and I didn't see eye to eye ever, at all."

3

Chuck and Rhonda

Christopher used to drag around this doll and Chuck didn't like it. "He doesn't need a baby," he said. I said, "Well, we'll make him some GI Joe clothes or something, but it's not going to hurt him to have a baby even though he's a boy."

E veryone seems to agree on what is most noteworthy about Chuck Attig because there are two things people always mention first: he's bald and he's adopted. "He had a hard life, he was adopted, and I can't imagine what that would be like to not know your real parents, and I'm sure that plays a major role in Chuck," says Robyn Carter earnestly. Of course, you can't tell from looking that he's adopted, so the importance of that fact in his life has been communicated by other than visual inspection. And you can't tell from looking that he's bald, because Chuck always wears a hat. In fact, Chuck only takes off his hat when compelled by a higher law — church or court. "He was so upset because he had to get married without his hat on," says Rhonda, who didn't know he was bald until she was already in love with him. She assured him that the hair loss "symbolized nothing." To help him be lighthearted about it, she smeared cake on his head at the reception. Debbie Phelps, who was initially attracted to him because of "the way he looked," didn't know he was bald until she visited him in jail, where he was serving a six-month sentence for domestic battery. "We'd known each other all that time and he'd never taken his hat off, at all," she recalls.

These stories can sound amusing from the distance of adulthood, but there's nothing funny about hair loss to an adolescent male, and as a severely myopic teenager with learning disabilities, Chuck already was self-conscious. Small wonder. The cruelty of adolescence is one reason why many people come to see the wisdom in the irreversibility of time. No one wants to relive the emotional and sexual confusion of the high school years. Perhaps, too, adolescent pecking is worse in a small town where little elbow room is permitted for difference and individuality and where every personal choice, foible, or blunder is broadcast live and up close on the merciless network of town opinion. All those mean teenagers learned their behavior from somewhere, after all.

Kevin Lockhart readily identified Chuck as "just a punk. All he could think about was fighting and being a badass." Drawing upon his own disreputable youth, Kevin thought that where he and his crowd seemed to get away with a lot, young toughs these days got looked over more carefully by local authorities, so Chuck "always ended up in jail, he didn't see the point, and well, Grandpa will buy me out, you know."

Chuck describes himself as "just somebody starting to grow up, a regular guy, for Murphysboro." By this, he allows as how he's a "hard character," and yet, not really.

"I pretend sometimes to be harder than I am. I don't like letting too many people in on my feelings and stuff because it seems like every time you do that, somebody always wants to step on you."

"I didn't think he was mean," says Debbie. At age thirty-seven, an established professional who works as a registered nurse in an OB unit, she saw potential beyond the bullying exterior. "He was very kind — and loud and funny. He's compassionate, and he was good with my children. I made sure he knew we were a package deal, and it was okay."

More than one person detected this appealing side to the inarticulate giant, because everyone is solicitous of Chuck, even as they reveal his mistakes and weaknesses. This sense of Chuck's embattled emotional condition is congruent with his long-range view of himself. "It seems like every time I try something, nothing seems to work. I either get halfway through it and decide not to do it or it blows up in my face or something goes wrong with it. That's why sometimes I got a scowl on my face and life just don't seem that grand," he says. He describes himself as more trusting of animals than humans, seeing himself in terms of the pit bull dogs he raises. "That's one thing that I look for in my dogs, you know, good spirit. You get a dog that has a broken spirit, you don't even want that dog no more because they're just not good for anything. I look back on myself and there have been so many times where my spirit has just about been broke, and makes me good for nothing."

Ruth might have been hard to please, Rhonda thought, and perhaps it was Chuck's "orphan," underdog status that appealed to her initially. Certainly she, too, was impressed with the hardship of his adoption. Rhonda was attracted to him because "he was just always there for me, he was always making me laugh." They met while partying with friends, and in Chuck's words, "We saw a lot of things in the same perspective, agreed on a lot of things, but then disagreed on a lot of things, so we just fell in love, I guess."

They lived together for a short time, and then, in a flurry of optimistic symbolism, Chuck proposed on Christmas Eve 1991. They got married on Valentine's Day 1992. Rhonda was twenty; Chuck was twenty-three. He worked at an auto parts salvage yard; Rhonda was a student at John A. Logan Community College. Ruth gave a reception for them at home, and they moved into a small apartment across the street from Ruth and Charlie Attig.

In retrospect, Chuck and Rhonda agree on at least one thing: neither one of them wanted to get married, but they did so to please Chuck's grandparents. "Whenever we were just living together, it was okay, because we didn't have any responsibilities, we just lived life day by day. But it went crazy," Chuck says.

"We were young and Chuck was wild and I was wild," says Rhonda.

Their whirlwind romance became "the whole married thing. You sit home and eat pizza and watch movies on Saturday night." Their whirlwind romance also became an abusive thing. Chuck may have been easy prey as a boy, but once he hit adolescence, he developed a handy weapon against every torment—his imposing physical presence. At six foot four and somewhere near two hundred pounds, with a remarkably deep voice, quick-tempered Chuck wouldn't need to do much more than growl and swat to make his wishes known. Only a month later, the marriage was already in trouble.

"They seemed happy at first, but Rhonda was going to school, and it's like she wouldn't let you get close to her, she was so close with her mother. She and Chuck would have a spat and she'd run home at the drop of a hat," Ruth recalls. Rhonda went back and forth between her mother's and her home with Chuck until she finally moved more or less permanently to Joyce's house in May 1992, the same month she applied for an Emergency Order of Protection under the Illinois Domestic Violence Act. The order cites death threats, public harassment, and physical violence dating back to March 1992.

"Chuck was obsessed with my sister," says Robyn. Like John Carter's insecurity with Joyce's schooling, Chuck was afraid of the competition, worried that Rhonda would find someone better in the college crowd. For her part, Rhonda didn't seem to mind yanking his chain by going out by herself and partying with friends. They argued over Rhonda's clothing, and Chuck's drinking, and about whether Chuck was seen talking to another woman, or Rhonda was seen talking to another man, and who stayed out all night and why.

"She'd call me and say she's never going to speak to him again, and then thirty minutes later her car would pull up over there and they'd be in bed. You know, I guess they liked the makeup after the fight, so they fought all the time so they could have the wonderful . . . " says Ruth, searching for the word that would anchor that sentence, explain what kept them together.

"So, we split up and then neither of us was sure if we wanted to split up, so it was a big hassle," Chuck says, summing up the chaotic early months of his marriage. One outcome of the drama and indecision that marked the union was that once the domestic protection order expired in June, Chuck moved into Joyce's house with Rhonda, who was pregnant with Christopher.

If living under the disapproving eye of Ruth was stressful for Rhonda, living with the Carter/Lockhart clan wasn't any easier for Chuck. "I see Chuck as somebody who really wants to fit in and doesn't always do so well," says Joyce, who determinedly emphasizes her affection for her menacing former son-in-law. "Chuck was adopted, and I learned a lot about his family life through Rhonda, and I developed a very special bonding with Chuck." Nonetheless, "I love Chuck, but if he was with Rhonda I would fear every day for her." There was a lot Joyce didn't see, perhaps because of her relentless optimism, perhaps simply because she worked full time and wasn't home to see what was going on. One of the events she didn't see, and didn't even hear about until Rhonda had moved in with Gary, was the time Chuck allegedly assaulted Rhonda when she was seven months pregnant.

Kevin and Joyce were gone, but Robyn and Buddy were hanging out in the front bedroom while Rhonda took a bath. Rhonda and Chuck had been fighting off and on all day about something stupid, as Rhonda recalled it, and he carried it into the bathroom. Screaming and hollering at her, Chuck ignored Rhonda's demands that he leave her alone. Rhonda was really stressed because they had been fighting a lot more than her parents knew, but she didn't want to go against her husband by telling her parents. Chuck was shouting and stalking back and forth between the bathroom and the adjacent bedroom.

"Come on, you guys, this is ridiculous," interjected Robyn from the bedroom where she was sitting with Buddy, but the shouting continued. And then, something Rhonda said pushed a last button. Chuck slammed the bathroom door shut and, holding the door tight, pushed Rhonda to the bottom of the tub. He let her up once.

"Don't do that again," she gasped, just before he pushed her under again.

"Oh my God," cried Robyn, as she and Buddy heard the sudden slip-swish of displaced water, and then Rhonda's struggled breath. Robyn jumped at the bathroom door, which Chuck was holding shut from the other side. As Rhonda bobbed back up, he rapped her sharply across the back of the head. Robyn jerked the door open to see her big-bellied sister floundering for her balance.

"My little brother was bawling, he didn't know what to do, and I didn't know what to do for him or for Rhonda," reports Robyn. But she went into action.

She sat right in the tub between Rhonda and the infuriated Chuck. "If you hit her again you're going to have to hit me too. She's pregnant! Calm down and leave, do whatever. But don't hit her anymore," pleaded Robyn.

"You better get out of my way, just get out of my way, or I'll get you too," he warned.

"Then deck me, because I'm not going nowhere, you know."

He backed off.

"I don't know what his intentions were; I think it was probably just to scare Rhonda. I don't think he was going to hurt her majorly or anything, but it scared me half to death," reports Robyn.

Several days later, Rhonda went into premature labor, and Christopher Michael Attig was born on December 7, 1992.

Rhonda was hospitalized for several days before Christopher was delivered, and she didn't see her son for forty-eight hours after he was delivered by an emergency cesarean section. Robyn had skipped classes to be with her sister, and she was sitting in the hallway waiting for news when a nurse ran through.

"What's going on?" Chuck demanded. The nurse stopped momentarily.

"It's a boy."

"Chuck was almost bawling," smiles Robyn, "and I knew he was thinking, 'I've got a son, I've got a son.'" Shortly thereafter, they wheeled Christopher by, and "oh, just the first sight was instant 'I love that baby.' He was so beautiful, so precious."

Rhonda was desperately ill, however, her undiagnosed preeclampsia now running its course as eclampsia. "She had seizures lasting seven to ten minutes, multiple seizures, and we thought at any minute we would lose her," says Joyce. "Our focus went from the baby on the ventilator back to Rhonda who would start seizing, back to Christopher, back to Rhonda." Joyce stayed with her daughter, and Chuck slept on the floor in her room for several nights.

Once Rhonda and Christopher were stabilized, both families visited continuously, each videotaping the infinitesimal daily growth of the first grandchild for each. At four pounds and four ounces, Christopher was so tiny the male nurse burped him with two fingers. Giant Chuck made the isolette look like a doll cradle as he gently reached in to change his son's diaper. "Hey, baby boy," he whispers on the tape. A wan, anxious Rhonda gazes at the camera, her eyes ringed with dark circles, face puffy and distorted from her recent ordeal. She looks nothing like the gamine girl of the family picture album. Chirping at the little boy, she offers him his first bottle. Ruth was there every day, stopping by before work, after work, and returning before she went to bed at night. At ten days, Christopher was an alert preemie, thin-faced and tiny, but working hard to open his eyes. "He actually had like rug burns on his knees and the top of his toes, because they had the isolette inclined, so he was scooting uphill. He was a fighter, and he made it," says Ruth, "only to have Gary Gould kill him."

Christopher outgrew all expectations and gained weight so rapidly that he was released to go home on December 21, a welcome Christmas gift for the anxious families. Flushed with fatherhood, Chuck bought Christopher a colorful outfit with dinosaurs on it, but before he could give it to the baby, he had to rip off the red bows on the front. His son would not wear bows!

Still exhausted from her near-fatal pregnancy and recovering from the C-section, Rhonda got a lot of help from her immediate family. Christopher had to be fed almost hourly and in very specific amounts, because overfeeding a premature baby could overwork the heart and cause congestive heart failure. Rhonda was so scrupulous about his health that she made visitors don a surgical mask, and she carefully observed the formula rationing schedule provided by the hospital. But Christopher had a hearty appetite, and although Rhonda began giving him more of his allotment at one time, he'd finish his day's allocation of formula before the day was over and wail for more. "I can't give him any more," Rhonda would protest, stricken by her son's hungry cries.

"So, I was always sneaking him some extra, and he just started growing like any baby would. You would never know he was a preemie," concluded Joyce.

Having a new baby in the house is exhilarating, but also utterly bone-wearying. If you are lucky, an infant might sleep through the night as early as six weeks, but most parents have found themselves sleep-deprived for much longer than that as they stagger through the seemingly endless rounds of feeding and changing and burping and crying. Days measured by the precious, hourly trivia of infant needs slide by so slowly, one indistinguishable from the next, it's difficult to see that the bottle, the baby, the diapers, and even the nights are all getting bigger, longer.

So, as Christopher knit his scrawny, premature self together into a round, lusty, fat-cheeked infant, Chuck and Rhonda fell apart. Tim Attig thinks that once Christopher was born, Chuck and Rhonda reversed roles. "Before that, it was she wantin' to have a family, and he was the one wantin' to be out all the time. But once she had a child, she was the one wantin' to be out all the time, and then my brother was the one trying to do good. It just seemed like she went off the deep end, and I've never known her to be that way before." Rhonda recommenced her young life. The mother who had scrupulously tended her baby, filled in every day for two months on his baby calendar, and taken him for all his early checkups missed his four-, six-, and twelve-month checkups, and minor childhood illnesses were often handled by a trip to the emergency room.

Although Ruth can be hard on Rhonda, she saw how Chuck and Rhonda were a match in their drive to have a good time. "I'm not saying it's all Rhonda, because they'd bring Christopher over here all the time [for us] to watch so they could go party." Ruth kept Christopher a lot on weekends, while Robyn and Joyce took responsibility for weekday care. "I just can't say no to anyone," Robyn says. So when Rhonda would ask her to take Christopher so she could go out, Robyn would say, "I just can't do this now. I have an exam tomorrow," and Rhonda would beg, "Please, please, please," and Robyn would give in. "Rhonda's my best friend," says Robyn. "She's a free spirit. She's very mature when she wants to be, and she's very loving, very caring. She has a great heart; she's a beautiful person, inside and out." Thus, while Rhonda was being free and "taking her chances to go out when they came," Robyn, with help from Joyce, became Christopher's primary caretaker for a good six months, roughly from February to July 1993.

Having a good time didn't seem to assist the marriage, however, for fighting continued as well. "When I grew up, my dad was mean to my mother, and I swore to myself I would never ever raise Christopher where he had to watch a man be mean to me, because that's a horrible thing," states Rhonda. Drinking seemed to incite Chuck, but sometimes he hit her when he was sober, once flat-handing her so hard she fell out of the rocking chair where she was holding Christopher. And then in early January, only a month after Christopher was born, the hostilities escalated.

As with most of the Rhonda and Chuck episodes, "she would have one story and he would have another and someone else who was there would tell you what really happened. So it's like they both only saw it their way," says Ruth. Rhonda, home caring for Christopher, was cranky and so tired that she was falling asleep trying to feed the baby. Chuck had stayed out all night and well into the next day, and Rhonda was furious. When he finally came home, she confronted him in the kitchen. "Where the hell have you been? We've got this little baby now, and I need you to help me. You can't be out runnin' around like this."

Chuck gave as good as he got. "You don't tell me what to do, and you don't holler and scream at me in front of your mom and everybody." He gave her a good shove to emphasize the point. When she pushed back, he lost his temper and, grabbing her by the back of the head, slammed her face into the edge of the upper kitchen cabinets.

Joyce was in the living room holding Christopher, so she only heard the yelling and then the thud as her daughter's face connected with hard wood.

"What's going on in there?" she yelled. She had the baby with her, and she was afraid to take him in there to check up on things.

Rhonda answered quickly, hoping to keep Joyce and Christopher and Robyn out of the kitchen. Most of the time when Chuck beat on her, her family wasn't around. He didn't do it when they would know. "Stay out of this, Mom." And then to Chuck, "Just leave. I don't feel like arguing with you, and it's better if you leave. Just go be with your friends, calm down, and come back whenever you're not going to be like that to me."

Apparently obeying her request, he stalked out of the kitchen, through the dining room, and down the hall to their room. He emerged a few seconds later with his new rifle in his hands. Rhonda, in the kitchen, and Robyn and Joyce, in the living room with Christopher, thought they heard him loading, muttering about shooting someone as he walked back into the kitchen.

Rhonda was scared to death. "Chuck, if you don't leave, I'm calling the police. You can't do this with the baby here and my mom and everyone."

"Don't worry, I'm leaving. I'm moving out." He grabbed the dog leash from the kitchen counter and stalked out.

"There wasn't even a gun on my part, no," says Chuck later. "Well, there was. She got me a gun for Christmas, and that's what the deal was on that. But it didn't even need to happen, because the squabble we got into was so minor. I was just goin' out to walk my dog and blow off some steam. There was no gun involved, but her mother, I guess, brought that in there."

"He borrowed $350 from us to buy Rhonda a Christmas present and then he went out and bought that rifle. Later I saw him at the mall, hassling Tim for some money so he could buy Rhonda some earrings. But maybe that's how they worked it out, you know, borrowing the money for him, not her. I'm not sure," says Joyce.

Joyce was quite sure, however, about how she felt that evening with the now-you-see-it, now-you-don't gun. She was angry and scared and she pushed Rhonda into calling the police and pressing charges of domestic battery against Chuck. Rhonda was mad enough to do it. She wanted to show him that she'd rather be alone than be treated that way, and she wanted him put in jail overnight to teach him that lesson.

But the incident brought a second charge against Chuck. He was just finishing a probationary period exacted for a guilty plea to the charge of ethnic intimidation. Possessing a firearm violated his probation. And while Rhonda cooled off quickly and refused to testify against him, the legal process set in motion by her complaint moved forward, both from its own momentum, because Robyn and Joyce stood firm in their resolve to press their part of the complaint, and because Chuck couldn't seem to leave well enough alone.

In February he was cited for violating bail by contacting Rhonda. In fact, it was their one-year wedding anniversary, and the complaint said he had contacted and harassed Rhonda Carter by following her throughout Murphysboro. Then about two weeks later, on March 2, Chuck showed up at Joyce's house with Rhonda, hoping to convince Joyce that she and Robyn didn't need to appear at the hearing, saying that if she testified, she would "have to answer to Terry Hickam." Chuck was threatening Joyce with a notorious Murphysboro bad boy, so Joyce returned the threat, responding that if he came on her property again, she'd have him arrested. She also had some harsh words for her daughter, who had reunited with Chuck. Rhonda couldn't have Christopher as long as she chose Chuck.

Rhonda and Chuck left without Christopher, but returned hours later, at 3:45 a.m. Robyn was at home, and while Chuck waited in the street, Robyn let Rhonda into the house and Rhonda took the baby, the diaper bag, and the formula, kidnapping her son from his grandmother.

Distraught and angry, Joyce stood screaming into the night, "You bring back my baby!"

"I'll chew you up and spit you out," Chuck promised her from his curbside safety.

"I'll see you in Menard," Joyce vowed back.

Rhonda's latest reconciliation with Chuck lasted only a short period, long enough for Ruth to lend her some clothing and Chuck some money to turn on the electricity so they could keep Christopher with them. They were living in a small apartment inside Terry Hickam's house. Sometimes Christopher slept in bed with them, but he also slept so often in his car seat that Ruth thought his head had started to flatten on the back. But Chuck's probation violation, attested to by Joyce and Robyn, dovetailed with the domestic violence charges. In April, Judge Watt found him guilty of violating his probation and sentenced him to six months in jail, and in May, Chuck pled guilty to domestic violence charges before Judge Kimberly Dahlen, who also sentenced him to six months in jail, to run concurrently with Judge Watt's sentence, with no day-for-day credit. In accord with the plea agreement, two other charges were dropped, a separate intimidation charge and the February harassment charge. Chuck went to jail for the second six months of Christopher's life. Rhonda, after hiding from her mother for a few days at Ruth's house, moved back home. Debbie Phelps and

Ruth visited Chuck in jail, bringing Christopher. Rhonda continued seeing Gary Gould.

Chuck had met Debbie and Rhonda had met Gary sometime in the first six months of Christopher's life. When Chuck began his six-month jail sentence in April/May 1993, Debbie sought him out, while Rhonda turned her full attention to Gary Gould. She got off work at 1:30 a.m. from her temporary bartending job, which gave her time to drive to Carrie's Place, which didn't close until 2:00 A.M., and have one drink and then go home. There she met Gary, who asked her out. She refused, saying that she didn't go home with people from bars. She insisted he call her at home for a date, which he did.

Compared to Chuck, Joyce thought Gary looked like a better choice for Rhonda. Even his Jackson County arrest record, which she wasn't aware of for some time, was modest, with only one felony conviction, for selling cocaine to an undercover agent. He didn't seem to beat on her, and Rhonda seemed happier. He sent her flowers, and they had a good time together, going to movies, eating out, riding motorcycles, and partying.

At twenty-seven, Gary was older than most of the men Rhonda went out with. Tall and well built with Fu Manchu facial hair and a biker costume, Gary cut a romantic figure to Rhonda. He was a member of the Phantoms, and he gave Rhonda a leather vest that said "Property of Tug." Biker men, however, are the property of no female, if local culture and *Easy Rider* magazine can be trusted. Even once Rhonda became "his," he usually had a woman on the side. Being with Rhonda had a distinct advantage, too. He had access to better wheels with which to visit the other women. Gary had a beat-up red pickup truck that he'd leave for Rhonda while he would take off in her Dodge Daytona. Kevin, who was working as a tow truck driver in Carbondale at the time, would come home and report that he'd seen this or that young woman driving Rhonda's car around town. Gary was generous with Rhonda's property, but when Kevin would comment on this to her, she'd get mad, because "she hates to be proven wrong in any way."

Although Chuck didn't mind using other kinds of drugs when they came his way, his primary drug was alcohol. Gary's drug use seems to have been more versatile — the usual alcohol, speed, and marijuana, as well as the more potent crack, crack-cocaine, and crank (methamphetamine). Joyce worried about Rhonda, who "is vulnerable. She likes to think of herself as a leader, but really she is a follower." From the beginning, the relationship with Gary was secured by drugs. Rhonda says that although she was acquainted with coke, she'd never even heard of crack until she met Gary. She found crack to be "powerful, addicting, an awful, awful drug." They were partying and smoking nightly in the early months of the relationship. "This is a horrible thing to have to tell people," but they were smoking so much "we started calling each other crackheads, and we got ourselves into debt really bad." But she emphasizes that Christopher wasn't with her then; he was staying with Robyn. Presumably, Rhonda and Gary ceased the crack habit once they moved in together.

Partying continued, however, as did Joyce and Kevin's concerns about Rhonda's new direction. But Joyce, worrying that she had perhaps interfered too much between Chuck and Rhonda, tried to moderate her counsel, fearing that if she was too negative, Rhonda would stop talking to her altogether and the lines of communication would break down. Rhonda, who describes herself as "a strong person, but I'm not really, I have to lean on somebody to be strong," was in no mood to heed parental cautions about her dashing new man.

"From the time I was fourteen, I was the worst child my mom and dad had," Rhonda confesses. "If Mom had said, 'Rhonda, I want you to stop partying with Gary Gould,' I'd have done the total opposite. I was a drug addict, and I didn't want to listen to anything she had to say. I thought I was on top of the world and my whole life was perfect and everything was peachy-keen, and I didn't have a problem, period."

And from that perspective, Gary Gould was her perfect companion. After a time, she began to think they might get married one day. Gary was "a charmer, a very free spirit," she says, "kind, wild, basically a pretty happy person all the time, except that he was a worrywart. He'd get stressed out if he forgot to call the insurance company, and worry about bills and things like that."

Being a free spirit, however, apparently he wasn't worried enough about bills to seek steady employment, preferring to live off his relatives and girlfriends. Like a lot of the young men he ran with, Gary Gould was intermittently employed. A high school graduate, he'd worked sporadically—as a nursing home attendant and later at Penn Aluminum, for a time. When Rhonda met him, he was living with his sister and brother-in-law, Beth and Matthew Merciez, and for several months, Rhonda visited him there. Later, he moved into his own apartment. The first night Gary slept over at Joyce's house with Rhonda, Christopher slept poorly. He kept sitting up and staring at Gary, unsure about the new man in the bedroom.

But no matter where Gary and Rhonda were living, they used Joyce's house as a daily base of operation, stopping by to eat breakfast and lunch, do the laundry, transfer Christopher, or pick up supplies. Although she bartended sporadically, Rhonda had gone on public aid shortly before Christopher was born, and much to Joyce's chagrin, she again quit college, seemingly unconcerned about her future or her unemployment. At first she had been using her public aid check to make her car payments, until she stopped even that, leaving her grandfather to foot the bill because he was the cosigner.

Although Joyce hadn't been that excited by Rhonda bartending, she thought Rhonda should work. Joyce was raised with a "very strong work ethic" and believes that "you get a lot more out of work than a paycheck." It seemed to her that Chuck and Gary were a bad influence on Rhonda, and she began to wonder about the source of Gary's income and what was happening to their money. She knew she was buying most of Christopher's diapers, although sometimes Gary would kick in for baby supplies or a toy. She found suspiciously large wads of money in the dryer.

From opposite ends of town, Ruth and Joyce, who never agreed on anything, suspected that Rhonda's public aid money was supporting illegal activities. Exhausted, Robyn began to bow out of continuous child care, and Ruth began to take up the slack. Debbie and Ruth continued visiting Chuck in jail, bringing his son, whom he couldn't hold, but only see. Christopher was learning to crawl.

Perhaps, given what is to come, I can be forgiven for tracing the shape of Christopher's death in the events of summer 1993. The summer itself was ordinary, a typical southern Illinois summer, when the humidity rivals the temperature, and even from inside the safety of an air conditioned building, you can anticipate its menacing embrace. At night, only the light changes, while the temperature stays where it is. Being straight means you have to face the heat every day. Getting wrecked means you can sleep through the worst of ordinary living, arising only with the humid creep of darkness across the light-flattened landscape.

The summer heat of southern Illinois is not an excuse or a reason, any more than drugs are an excuse or a reason, but merely context: the environmental megaphone that may have assisted the unfolding tragedy. The marriage and Chuck's dog, Slick, died one summer, and Christopher died the next.

Rhonda filed for divorce and custody of Christopher on July 1, 1993, and three days later, Slick died of something resembling heatstroke. Rhonda had been taking care of the black pit bull for her jailbound husband. Slick was tied up on a short chain in the sun in front of the garage at Joyce's house. There was a doghouse, but no shade, and it was a blistering Fourth of July. That afternoon, while the family was attending a car show, Slick perished, dying in convulsions as they returned from the afternoon recreation.

The death of Slick was symbolically important, coinciding as it did with the end of the marriage. For Chuck, it was devastating, because Christopher and Slick were the "only two things in the world he really had," says Tim. Tim wonders whether they "just quit caring for the dog," which as far as he knew was "healthy as could be."

"They said he had a heatstroke, but I think someone poisoned him," says Rhonda. "He had water in his bowl. I felt so terrible. I knew how he felt about that dog—I loved it to death."

Although the divorce was not finalized for several months, Rhonda was safe from her abusive husband, free to enjoy her young life again. Always something of a night owl, her bartending and then her partying plunged her into the "crazy nights of Gary," a summer of hot, reckless self-pleasuring that devoured all perspective and order, and finally, a year later, the life of her son.

4

Where Was Christopher?

He came running to the door and he had on this big som-
brero and he was just in a diaper. He looked at me with that
little grin of his and wiggled the brim of the hat, flopped
around, and zoom, off he went.

I n the beginning, she did love Christopher, but once she met Gary
Gould I think she forgot what love was," says Ruth, still struggling
to understand how Rhonda could have traded the baby for the
biker.

Ironically, Ruth got to keep Christopher far more often than she
would have had Rhonda been acting more like Christopher's full-time
mother, and for Ruth, the opportunity to keep Christopher was always
welcome. Robyn and Joyce stepped in for Rhonda as long as they could,
but Robyn was working and going to school full time, and Joyce was
putting in long hours at the hospital. Both were exhausted, and not a
little exasperated. Alarmed at how seldom Rhonda was seeing Christopher, Joyce told her she was missing all of Christopher's important de-
velopmental milestones and that it was time for her to start caring for
her own baby. Rhonda's response was to take Christopher to Ruth's
more frequently, so her mother still didn't know if Rhonda was seeing
any of the wonderful things Christopher was learning and doing.

According to the divorce decree, Chuck got Christopher on alternating weekends and holidays and for the month of July. At first, Ruth

got Christopher on the alternate weekends, filling in for Chuck, but by early fall 1993, Rhonda began bringing him by in the middle of the week, and Ruth would have him on Tuesday and Wednesday, Rhonda would take him on Thursday, and Ruth would get him back for Friday, Saturday, and Sunday, including Sunday night. Rhonda knew that she could always call Ruth, because "she always, always wanted him. So I always called her. She worked really well with me from the beginning, and she was never rude to me." Rhonda liked it that Ruth took Christopher to Sunday school, and she knew Christopher loved being with Maw Maw. "Ruth was his favorite, above all," says Rhonda. "I love my mother, and she was wonderful with Christopher, but she had her career and my little brother and sister to look after, too. When I took Christopher to Ruth's, I knew he had 175 percent attention there."

What was a satisfactory arrangement for Rhonda, however, was fraught with anxiety for Ruth, who found it difficult to adapt to the unreliable schedule of her former daughter-in-law. Rhonda got into the habit of dropping Christopher with Ruth and then not showing up to reclaim him at the agreed-upon time. "One night she just knocked on the door and Christopher was asleep in the truck, and they wanted to go to a dance bar, her and a couple of girls," Ruth recalls.

"Can you keep Christopher for a couple of hours?" Rhonda asked.

"Of course," Ruth responded.

"I'll be back after him about eleven o'clock; will that be too late?"

"No, that will be fine."

She never came back that night.

The morning following such a drop-off, if it was a workday, Ruth would call Joyce's, looking for someone to take over so she could go to work. But it was hard to raise anyone there. Joyce was off to work early, and Rhonda was sleeping, not to be disturbed until afternoon. Whether bartending or partying, she pleaded that she was too wiped out to get up and care for her son in the mornings. So, if Ruth couldn't get someone at the Carter/Lockhart household, Tim would volunteer to miss classes and stay with Christopher. He, too, would call at Joyce's, hoping he could at least make afternoon classes.

By October 1993, Christopher was walking, Chuck was out of jail, and Ruth gave up trying to get Rhonda to reclaim her son. If Rhonda didn't return for him and Ruth had to work, Christopher would go stay with Chuck, who was working nights, and Debbie, who was also working full time and caring for her two children. They kept a portable crib, clothing, and diapers on hand, and Christopher shared a room with Debbie's seven-year-old.

But Ruth wasn't just concerned about her own uneasiness with Christopher's traveling child care; she also worried about the effect on him. Christopher was on an erratic sleeping schedule, sometimes not dozing off until five in the morning. On those nights, Tim would spell his mother, giving her a chance to get a few hours' sleep before going to work. Sometimes it was up to Ruth to deliver Christopher to his next caretaker, and Rhonda would specify an exact time. Ruth vividly remembers a miserable winter day when she had arranged to return Christopher before she went to work that morning. When she got to Joyce's house, she got the sleeping baby out of his car seat, bundled him up in a blanket, and went to the door. She knocked and knocked, but no one answered, so she had to load him back up and take him home. Once home, she called Chuck and Debbie, who immediately agreed to take him. So, she bundled him back up again and loaded him in the car. But by then, he was awake, and "when I left, he cried and put out his arms to me and I felt like a terrible grandmother to have to leave him."

"Even though I partied all the time, I was with him every day that he was in this house," says Rhonda, referring to Christopher's time at Joyce's house. "I didn't do things like I should have done, and I regret that, but he was always taken care of," whether by Ruth, Robyn or Joyce; "otherwise I wouldn't have been partying like I was."

It's easy to locate fault with Rhonda as the custodial parent who was neither employed nor in school. She went days without seeing her son. But once Chuck got out of jail, where was he? Well, he was particular about how Christopher was handled and gave Rhonda instructions about his expectations. But when Chuck had Christopher, he would bring him back to Ruth much earlier than he was supposed to, and many weekends, when Chuck knew Christopher was with Ruth, he was too busy to stop by to see his son. That's why Ruth doesn't have very many pictures of Chuck with Christopher and why Tim is in all the videos.

With some hope for custody, Ruth tried to work out a day-care situation for Christopher for those times when she had to work, assuring Rhonda that she could have Christopher any time she wanted. But Rhonda didn't want to put him into day-care until he was old enough to talk, so that he could tell if someone was hurting him, and unlike day-care children, Christopher was usually being cared for by a family member, which was an important point for Rhonda and Chuck. Eventually, Rhonda came to see Gary as a family member.

What Joyce liked about Gary was that "he was funny, he could tell a joke. When you would see [him] and Rhonda and Christopher interact on a good day, there was just love and laughter between them." At first, though, she thought he was cold, because on an early visit he refused interaction with Christopher. For forty-five minutes the curious child crawled all over Gary's legs and messed with his biker boots, becoming more and more insistent in his gambol for attention. Gary pretended he wasn't there. "It just broke my heart, because no one had ever walked into this house and ignored Christopher like that."

But Joyce's reservations were lulled, for she thought she saw Gary warm up to the child as time went on, and she felt Gary genuinely cared for the little boy. Rhonda thought Gary was good with Christopher, too. "He played with Christopher and changed him, and bathed him, and took him with him whenever he was running here or there, and babysat him all the time." As per her agreement with Chuck, Gary was not allowed to physically discipline Christopher, but in all other ways, "he helped me take care of him like a stepparent would."

This picture of Gary Gould is certainly congruent with Rhonda's initial experience of him as a nice guy who brought her flowers. And yet, somewhere along the line, he revealed another side of himself, and she became confused about which one "was the real Gary." Joyce wondered if he wasn't trying to drive a wedge between herself and Rhonda, presenting a smiling face to her but behind her back urging Rhonda to flout her wishes or to keep secrets from her. Joyce also wondered if Gary was trying to separate Rhonda from Christopher, and even Rhonda wondered if Gary was jealous of her son. She knew he was sometimes irritated by Christopher, because Rhonda couldn't just pick up and go riding and partying, a pastime not readily adaptable to the needs of an active toddler.

Christopher celebrated Christmas 1993 twice that year, first with Rhonda's family, then, arriving about 9:00 P.M., with the Attigs. He's listless as Ruth's tape begins, both sleepy and tired from a minor cold. But he brightens up as Uncle Tim begins to play with him. With his big brown eyes, a whisper of gold down on his head, and his immense fat cheeks, he is a beautiful little boy, utterly adorable as he concentrates on putting things into boxes and containers and shaking the invented rattle vigorously. He works his eyebrows as he plays and vocalizes about it all. Down on his hands and knees, Uncle Tim answers him. Together they follow the Tooneyville Choo Choo Train around the kitchen floor, big boy and little boy calling and responding in happy baby syllables. Doo-ah. GA, GA. EEEEEEHHH. Christopher puffs out his cheeks, trying to make train noises.

While Christopher was demonstrating all the appropriate behavioral markers for his age, the same could not be said for Gary. His behavior at Christmas did nothing to allay Joyce's "gut instinct that there was something very self-centered and selfish about Gary."

That year Kevin had gotten a windfall, and because Christmas is her favorite time of year, Joyce went all-out on presents for her family. Christopher got so many toys that Rhonda spread them out on the bed and took a group photo. You can't see the bed underneath, and in one picture, it's easy to miss Christopher himself, enthroned amidst his treasures. Joyce included Gary in her gift giving, buying him, among other things, jeans and a Harley t-shirt and some cologne. "Gary accepted it gracefully, although I think he felt that I had bought Rhonda too much." Rhonda's big gift from Joyce was a papasan chair. Gary didn't buy Rhonda anything, or anyone else for that matter. Why?

Because he's an atheist, Rhonda told her mom, and don't ever buy him things anymore.

Joyce thought Gary was feeding Rhonda a line, but she didn't say anything out loud, afraid that Gary was influencing Rhonda not to come around, and then she wouldn't bring Christopher, and Joyce didn't want that to happen. As it was, she was seeing less and less of her willful daughter, because around Christmas 1993–January 1994, Rhonda moved with Gary to an isolated trailer lot off a rural blacktop. One of four units, the trailer looks across the gravel road at a cornfield, with pastureland and soybeans on either side. There, Gary and Rhonda had a more discreet location in which to continue their partying.

If being stood up by Rhonda was a dismaying experience, connecting with Rhonda for child transfer wasn't much more reassuring once Ruth began to deliver the child to Rhonda's new home with Gary at the trailer. On one occasion, Rhonda called for Ruth to bring Christopher. When Ruth arrived, Rhonda was on the phone. Overflowing ashtrays, beer cans, and glasses with tepid sloshes of liquid in them seemed to cover every surface. Christopher saw this as a great opportunity to practice his retrieval and dump skills, and like all toddlers, his mouth was the first organ consulted for new tactile experiences. So, while she waited for Rhonda to get off the phone and bulldog her son, Ruth followed the active child around the trailer, rescuing glasses and ashtray garbage from inquisitive fingers and lips. "She called me to bring him home. Why didn't she clean up a little?" This wasn't just a matter of differing standards of cleanliness. Rhonda had told her that one morning Christopher had awakened early and climbed up on the dresser, snagging the cigarettes from the night before. They didn't know how many he ate, but he "puked and puked and puked."

In that spring of 1994, Christopher was an active, healthy toddler, and his family delights in recalling his exploits. Debbie Phelps remembers his "really strong belly laugh," and Christopher's expressions reminded her of Chuck, "especially the ornery expressions, when he's being a little devil and teasing." Robyn recalls that Christopher had a little four-wheeler that he couldn't ride very well, but "he'd get out by the ditch and turn around and we'd yell, 'Christopher, you're not supposed to be out there, get back here,' and he'd just push that little button to make it go more!" At Joyce's house, Rhonda would "throw him on the waterbed and the bed would go crazy and he'd be all happy and he'd stand up and run over and want to do it again." He loved riding on the vacuum cleaner and delighted in teasing Joyce by taking down the gate at the end of the hall; "he always made sure you were looking at him so you would know he was aggravating." Rhonda smiles at a picture of Christopher standing in the clean laundry basket with Kevin's underwear on his head, and another where he's grinning, about to eat a forbidden blue jelly bean.

He loved to play in Charlie's workshop in the sawdust, or get sprinkled by Uncle Tim with the shower water. He would rummage around in Tim's things, and Tim obliged him by keeping "an empty bottle for him to think he was getting into something bad but he really wasn't." When Tim was working out in the yard, Christopher would get underneath the car or truck with him and pick up a wrench and help, "and we'd just stop what we were doing so we could play," Tim recalls. Ruth discovered that he could get his arm down into the child-proofed cabinet below the counter, and he'd leave his pacifier behind when he was successful in grabbing graham crackers. "When I'd give him a bath," Ruth says, "I'd flip his hair upwards and I always thought he looked like a little Kewpie doll running around the house in his bare bottom."

Clearly, Christopher was past the age when he could be plopped in a playpen or strapped in a carrier. He took a lot of falls that spring, including a harmless plunge down Joyce's basement stairs, and his medical records show several trips to the emergency room or the doctor to check out this or that head bump. Some observers mention that he seemed to be bruised a lot, but there's no way of knowing whether his bruising was excessive or part of the normal bumps and dents of toddlerhood. Gary reported that Christopher was "accident-prone," but there was nothing unusual about Christopher except that he was probably not watched as closely as he might have been, or he was being watched by someone with a short fuse. It's about this time that Christopher shows up with the finger prints on his face and a strange red welt across his neck and chest, the latter injury variously attributed to falling on a flyswatter or being clawed by the dog, the former injury owned by no one.

Gary Gould was charming, and those who found him congenial company saw him as a good-time guy who did his share of the child care when asked. Robyn thought he was "very good with Christopher," although it seemed to her that Gary ought "to get out of the business that he's in," namely, drug dealing, because it is a "very high-stress career choice." Beth Merciez, Gary's sister, testified in court that she had no problem leaving her two small children in Gary's care. From most appearances, Gary seemed to care about Christopher. Understandably, Joyce and Rhonda felt better thinking so.

Those less invested in enumerating his good points, however, offer disturbing counterimages of "the other Gary" whom Joyce detected in moments of slippage. Ruth mentions witnessing Gary's temper, just in the brief encounters she had while returning or picking up Christopher. She thought he was "violent and explosive, and if he said something, he wanted you to do it right now or ten seconds before he thought of it." Rhonda recalls Gary telling Beth that sometimes when he's fighting, he has blackouts, loses control, and has no idea what he's doing. Given these reports, it becomes more alarming to find one trailer park neighbor who remembers Gary carrying three guns around, anticipating some kind of unspecified trouble, and he thought Gary acted paranoid, like something was going on all the time. This wouldn't be surprising, for although she is notably vague on what Gary was doing with the guns, Rhonda reported that guns were regularly coming in and out of the trailer.

Other brief glimpses of life at the small, isolated trailer court mentioned in common by Rhonda and Gary's neighbors and others include the three- to four-day Memorial Day party of 1994 (a social event that seemed to involve lots of intoxicants, damage to nearby farm equipment, and drunken people running amok through the neighboring cornfield), their unanimous distaste for Terry Hickam as a reason why they kept contact with Gary to a minimum, and a loud argument between Gary and Rhonda about Rhonda throwing away a bag of Doritos. One neighbor recalled with disgust the day he saw Gary and Terry Hickam siccing their pit bull on a cat. As the two men shouted encouragement, the dog shook the cat to pieces. Several people described the atmosphere as "not conducive to raising a child." Apparently there was little routine, and while all sorts of people came and went at odd times of the day and night, Christopher and other young children visiting might be left unsupervised to play for long periods of time.

Sometimes the neighbors could hear a child crying in the night, which in and of itself is hardly significant. Young children often don't sleep well, nor do they always comfort readily. No one saw much of Christopher. One tenant said it was a long time before he even knew there was a child living there, and another tenant could only remember seeing Rhonda and Christopher outside once during the six months they had occupied the front trailer.

What we know about Gary Gould is that in high school he played sports and sang in chorus, but his life after graduation wasn't promising. He was carrying drugs and guns out of the trailer, periodically unemployed, prone to temper tantrums, and not very selective about his companions. He was a biker who used and dealt drugs, enjoyed a good time, could tell a good story, and liked to dominate and exploit women. He was a man whom some people trusted as a baby-sitter and who was capable of being nice to children. Does all this add up to a personality capable of killing a child?

Not necessarily. According to one withering assessment of Gary's character, Gary couldn't have hurt Christopher, because Gary only cares about himself. If Christopher had been aggravating Gary that morning by crying or whining, he would have just turned up the stereo to drown the child out.

Once out of jail, Chuck tried to keep tabs on Gary and Christopher, and friends reported to him that Gary was okay with his son. But Chuck was also hearing that things were not okay with Rhonda, and he confronted her about why she was always leaving Christopher and about the things that were going on out at the trailer. "I think I even said that people were watching her, trying to get it into her head that Christopher needed some more attention from her, and she went and told Gary I had somebody watching them."

This made Gary furious, and one June day Chuck and Gary squared off. Chuck had just pulled up to Joyce's house in his Bronco with Christopher in the front seat. Before Chuck had a chance to get the boy out of the truck, Gary came charging out of the house, angry and poking at him, using every cuss word you could think of.

"You worry about Christopher whenever you have Christopher,

and don't worry about things whenever Christopher is with me and Rhonda," Gary shouted.

"I'll worry about Christopher whenever, all the time, because he's my boy, twenty-four/seven. Don't ever cross me on my boy, or you'll answer to me," Chuck retorted.

While the two men were scratching up the dirt, getting sweaty, and barking "cunt" back and forth at each other, Christopher sat goggle-eyed in the truck.

"When I looked out," says Joyce, "all I could see was here was Christopher watching this, and he dearly loved his daddy, and Gary who he also loved, there they were, screaming at each other." As Rhonda wept, Joyce dashed outside and retrieved Christopher, who seemed unscathed, "but you know he heard everything, and I know he could interpret the emotions."

"And that's what just tears me up," says Chuck. "If only I'd done something right then and there and made the issue [of Christopher's child care] more public instead of what I did."

What Chuck did was accept an invitation to be recruited for the Phantoms, presumably a way to keep him in closer contact with Gary and Rhonda and Christopher, but perhaps, he thinks in retrospect, also a way to make him an accomplice to the life-style he was criticizing. Always something of a biker "wannabe," Chuck was not averse to being "prospected" by the motorcycle club. It was a way to belong—and keep tabs on Christopher, he rationalized.

Since getting out of jail in October, Chuck had been working to build his relationship with his son. It hurt him that Christopher would cry and squirm around, looking for Debbie or Ruth whenever Chuck would try to hold him, but Chuck was patient and didn't push himself on the skeptical little boy. Gradually, Christopher got to know his father and would come to him when Chuck put out his arms, and "that made me so happy. He was a lot like me, you know, he didn't want to trust right away, but then whenever he did, he'd trust fully."

Chuck and Debbie set up a special shelf in the refrigerator with his drinks and snacks, and Chuck "made him a lot of stuff that was real messy and just let him eat it the way he wanted."

"I'd sit him up on the counter and let him see what I was making and then he'd get all excited and happy because he knew whenever it cooled off that he was going to get to tear into it." As he bonded with his daddy, Christopher learned to play with the dogs, and Chuck would take them to the park, letting the happy toddler chase around after the accommodating animals. That summer of 1994 looked promising to Chuck. Although he was still running afoul of the law periodically, he managed to stay out of jail. He was employed, involved in a stable relationship, and was getting to know and enjoy his son.

Chuck had custody of Christopher that July, although because of his night work schedule as a welder and Debbie's day job as an RN, Ruth still kept Christopher most of the time. Still, Chuck became more and more secure in his new role, and he began to look forward to the future. "It was a pick-me-up when Christopher and me had everything going. I could just tell it was going to get better and better, having plans, you know, talking about buying big swing sets and above-ground pools." It was scary being a dad, but Chuck liked it. "He was mine, he was part of me, and I could just watch him grow up and tell him things that my dad told me. I was just looking forward to being able to raise him. I could tell he was going to be so high-spirited that he wasn't going to have the downs that I had. He was just going to step over them."

Thursday, July 28, 1994. As that happy, hectic month drew to a close, Christopher returned to Joyce's house for a day or two so they could take him to a family gathering. One of the last times Robyn saw him was on that Thursday morning. She picked him up from Ruth's and took him back to the house to watch him while she got ready to meet Rhonda that afternoon, although Christopher was making it difficult.

He kept eating her cigarettes. "He was a little superman, that's what he was," she says. "I don't care if they were up on top of the ceiling fan, he'd find a way to get them."

She nabbed him and plopped him on the couch to watch cartoons, but five minutes later, there he was again with her cigarettes. He was chomping and sucking on them, and there were little slobbers of tobacco flakes everywhere.

"Christopher," she yelled. "I don't have any money left, and that's all my cigarettes." She cleaned him up and set him on the couch again. "Okay," she yelled, still angry, "you have to sit here and watch TV until I get done getting ready."

Christopher looked at her like, "Yeah, Aunt Robyn, I'm going to make you miserable." And then he sat perfectly still, with his lip stuck out, crying, and he watched cartoons for fifteen minutes.

Robyn was amazed. You could never get Christopher to sit still like that. "Oh man, now he's really upset," she thought. "He's not going to come to me or anything." So she sat down beside him and said, "I'm sorry, Christopher." And then it occurred to her that she was apologizing to a one-and-a-half-year-old, and she began to laugh.

"It's pretty bad when a baby can get to you like that, but he was so smart, he knew how to do it." She took him to Huck's and bought him a sucker, and then they went to meet Rhonda.

That evening, Joyce returned to the house with Christopher. The family had scattered in pursuit of various plans, and it was the first time she'd been alone in that house in quite a while, so she was glad for his company. It was virtually her last time alone with Christopher. They went to bed together, but Christopher awakened early the next morning, around 5 A.M. She followed him into the kitchen. Standing and pointing at the cabinet where they kept his bottles, he said, "Mama babaa [bottle], Mama babaa." It was the first time Joyce had heard him put two words together. She didn't have any milk in the house, and she knew that Debbie and Chuck had taken him off the bottle. But she had never been in a hurry to take the bottle away from her children, and she couldn't see that it would hurt now. So she fixed him a bottle of cherry Kool-Aid and took him back to bed with her. They slept peacefully together until it was time for Joyce to get up. She dropped Christopher off at Gary and Rhonda's trailer before going on to work.

Friday, July 29, 1994. There is a sweet picture of Christopher with his uncle Buddy, sitting in the back seat of the car. Buddy is curving his head sideways over Christopher, who gazes at the camera calmly, secure in the circle of his young uncle's attention. They are on their way with Rhonda and Robyn to see *The Lion King.* Christopher wasn't that interested in the movie, although he'd take notice when the singing started, and then he'd be ready to run around the theater again. He ate two little popcorns, so they got a big bucket and Christopher helped devour that, too. "He'd get two handfuls and just keep shoving it into his mouth. He really liked popcorn," remembers Rhonda. That was the last time Buddy saw Christopher alive.

Rhonda took Christopher back to Chuck and Debbie sometime that day. Christopher was in good spirits, and Debbie remembers him playing with one of Chuck's hats and high-stepping around the kitchen in circles singing, "Na na na na na." He spent the night there. The next morning, Chuck cooked Christopher a big batch of spaghetti for breakfast and let him have at it, so when Ruth came to pick him up, Christopher looked like a big, happy meatball, covered with spaghetti sauce. He may have spent a few hours with Rhonda during that day, but he spent the night at Ruth's, so she could take him to Sunday school the next morning, before returning him to Rhonda's custody.

Sunday, July 31, 1994. Ruth got Christopher up early on Sunday mornings so she could take him to Sunday school. Several weeks earlier, there had been a peculiar incident there. Christopher had grabbed a little girl by the shoulders and, teeth bared in a terrible grimace, shook her fiercely. He was gripping her so hard they had to pry his fingers from the fabric of her dress. At the time, Ruth wondered where he'd seen such behavior, but it wasn't until later that the incident took on an awful significance.

Although she felt guilty about skipping church, she usually didn't stay, because she didn't want to leave Christopher in the church nursery. On this particular morning, she had no choice about staying, because Rhonda told her they wanted to pick him up promptly at 10:30 A.M. to go to lunch with an uncle who was in town. She specified that he was to be clean and dressed in his Lion King outfit and that Ruth was not to feed him after breakfast.

Literalist that she was, Ruth hurried home with Christopher, arriving home right on time. Rhonda didn't come and didn't come.

About 11:15 A.M., Christopher was getting fussy, so Ruth called the trailer. A house guest answered the phone. She hollered at Rhonda, and then there was a groany sound in the background.

"Rhonda can't come to the phone right now," she said.

"This is Ruth. Rhonda was supposed to be here at 10:30, and I can't hold him off any longer. Christopher is tired and hungry, so I'm going to feed him and put him down for a nap."

"Um, she'll call you back in half an hour."

"Well, she needn't bother. I'm going to feed Christopher, and he'll nap for at least two hours. She can call after that."

A half an hour later Rhonda called, sounding so spacey she could hardly put a sentence together. Ruth repeated that Christopher had just finished eating and was falling asleep. The last picture of Christopher with his Paw Paw, an uncanny parallel with the picture taken just two days earlier with his uncle Buddy, records that moment. As Ruth was cleaning up the kitchen from lunch, Charlie sat back in a comfortable chair and Christopher nestled in on his chest, his head tucked under his Paw Paw's chin, drowsy eyes at the camera, content, safe in the watchful curve of a loving big person.

Rhonda reported that she was waiting for a ride but would definitely be there by 2:00 P.M. But two o'clock came and went. Up from his nap and still in his Lion King outfit, Christopher went out to play, first in the back of Paw Paw's truck and then in the big dirt pile in Maw Maw's front yard.

Rhonda showed up at 4:30 that afternoon and took him away. It was the last time Ruth and Charlie saw him alive.

Monday, August 1, 1994. Joyce saw Christopher only briefly on Monday, when Gary stopped by to change his diaper. That afternoon Beth's little boy came over to play at the trailer and Gary took care of the two youngsters while Beth and Matt kept an appointment in town. Gary and Rhonda noticed Christopher pulling on his ear, and he seemed a little whiny. But he was eating and playing as usual, so there didn't seem to be any medical emergency involved. Sometime during that day, Rhonda stopped by her mother's house, and to Joyce's dismay announced a new plan: she was going to get a job bartending or waitressing while Gary waited for a settlement from a motorcycle accident in July. If he got a job, the insurance company would catch on that he could work, so Rhonda would become the breadwinner and Gary would sit with Christopher. Acting on an impulse, Joyce spoke out: "Rhonda, please don't let Gary baby-sit Christopher. I don't care if you go back to work, but I have a terrible feeling about him baby-sitting." The next time Joyce saw Christopher, he was dying.

Tuesday, August 2, 1994. Rhonda spent the day cleaning her grandmother's house, so Gary spent another day with Christopher. Later in the afternoon, Gary took the boy to Beth's house, where Christopher and Beth's children chowed down on fruit snacks and played with trucks until it was time for Gary to pick Rhonda up. Christopher was still pulling on his ears.

They drove to Carbondale and had dinner at Taco John's. Rhonda discovered that Christopher loved mexirolls, and he ate a big dinner. She'd tied a handkerchief on his head with the two tails hanging down, just like his dad, who always wore some sort of head covering. On the way home, Christopher stood in her lap, sticking his head out the window. "The little tails on his handkerchief were just blowing in the wind, and he had his eyes squinted shut, and he was just laughing, laughing, laughing. Gary kept saying, 'I can't believe how much he looks like his father.'" For a moment, they were happy together with the gleeful little boy with the wind in his face.

The camaraderie was short-lived, however. Joyce phoned the trailer sometime that evening. In the background, Gary was screaming something about "leave that alone, get away from that." Rhonda told her he was yelling at the dog, but Joyce thinks he was yelling at Christopher. Gary left Rhonda at the trailer at 6:00 P.M. and went out. He came back at ten o'clock and they fought, and he left again.

Furious at being excluded from the good time she thought Gary must be having, Rhonda smoked a joint, watched TV with Christopher, and smoldered. Gary returned around 2:00 A.M. He'd been to JB's, a bar and strip joint, partying and catching up with old girlfriends. They fought some more, not a "'fight'-fight," just "screaming and yelling at each other," and then they went to bed about 3:30 in the morning. Where was Christopher? Christopher was asleep on the couch in the living room.

5

August 3–4, 1994

August 3, 1994 was like any other southern Illinois summer day, with the thermometer hitting the mid-eighties and the heat compounded by a suffocating humidity. Trailer living looks especially oppressive in the heat. Even if you know it's air conditioned, as Gary and Rhonda's trailer was, there is something about all that white, glary metal burning in the sun-raked fields that broadcasts an ominous portent.

After a short night, Gary got up about seven the next morning to run some errands in town. Christopher was still sleeping on the living room couch, and Gary moved him into the bedroom with Rhonda, who was also still sleeping.

Gary returned about 9:30 A.M. with a bag of breakfast burritos. Rhonda got up with Christopher and, because she was running late, took a bath with him. She was getting ready to go to town to put in job applications and run some errands in Carbondale. While she was getting dressed, Gary diapered Christopher and fed him some breakfast, part of a burrito and a Pop-Tart. As they were eating, a friend of Gary's from Penn Aluminum stopped by to buy some crank and drink a beer, but Rhonda was pretty sure Gary wasn't using drugs that morning because he didn't usually eat when he did drugs.

Although he was up and about, Christopher seemed whiny and was still pulling on his ear, and Rhonda figured that perhaps they should take him to the doctor to get medicine for his earache. They called Beth Merciez, and she put her little boy on the phone to talk to Christopher, hoping that would soothe him. After a second phone call, arrangements were made for Christopher to play with Beth's children later that morning. Rhonda was using Gary's truck to go into town, so Beth agreed to come by and get Christopher and take him to her house.

As she got ready to leave, Rhonda considered taking Christopher with her. Maybe she could drop him off at Ruth's. Christopher always cried when she left, and he was crying and clinging to her once he saw her gathering her keys and purse to leave. But Gary seemed impatient with her indecisiveness.

"Go, just leave him here, go ahead and go do it." Well, she thought, maybe he was just being understanding about her not wanting to take her toddler on a job interview. Still, it bothered her a little. Gary had never insisted so much on her leaving Christopher with him. Then she decided she was just being silly. Gary had kept Christopher many times before, and things had always worked out fine. She knew that Christopher loved Gary, and the boy was working hard on saying "Gary's truck," because he loved to go when Gary was running errands. And Gary seemed to care about Christopher, too, even waking in the night to take care of him when he was restless or sick.

Rhonda left sometime between 10:30 and 11:30 A.M. Still crying, Christopher stood in the doorway of the trailer, waving bye-bye to Mommy.

Not too long after the second phone call arranging a play time for

Christopher, perhaps a little after 12:00 noon, Beth Merciez received a
third phone call. It was Gary. He was so loud and incoherent that Beth
at first thought he was laughing.

"Something bad has happened to Christopher. You've got to get out
here right now," he finally managed to convey.

"Are you serious?" she asked, still not sure she was understanding
what he was saying.

"I'm serious," he choked out. "Get out here fast."

Without asking any questions, Beth "took off out the door." When
she arrived at the trailer, she saw Christopher lying on the couch, his
head propped up on the arm of the couch, covered in a blanket. Beth
whisked the blanket off him and picked him up. He was dressed in a
clean diaper. What she saw horrified her. "He was drawing hisself, he
would just stiffen his arms and legs out and kind of curl his toes and his
fingers," convulsing every few seconds.

As Gary paced about the living room, Beth held him close and said,
"Wake up, Christopher, wake up," but she knew he wasn't waking up.
His eyes were closed, but when the lids fluttered open, she could see
his eyes rolling in his head. And the awful seizures continued their terrible perfect rhythm.

"We've got to get him to the hospital," she commanded, and still
holding the stricken child, she ran out to her Bronco. Gary drove.
Christopher was so stiff and unresponsive that Beth, who couldn't
weigh more than ninety pounds all wet, had trouble holding onto him.
At thirty-five pounds, nineteen-month-old Christopher had topped the
ninety-fifth percentile in weight. Beth struggled to hold his head up
and keep him on her lap as they careened to the hospital, his solid little
body now a dead weight. He was bleeding from the mouth.

They hadn't talked much in the trailer, but now Beth filled the short
ride to the hospital with questions.

"What happened, Gary?" she demanded.

"We were outside," he said. "Playing with the hose and the four-wheeler. Then we came in so I could change his pants 'cause they got wet, and he wanted a drink. And then he just collapsed and fell on his face. He cried a little, and then his head just started bobbin' around and his eyes rolling this horrible way."

"Think, Gary. Do you remember doing anything to him at all?"

"No, no, I didn't do anything. I just, like, put a washrag on his neck to cool him off, and then laid him on the couch and covered him up."

"Could he have gotten into anything," she asked, "like drugs, or medicine, or cleaning stuff?"

"I'm telling you, I don't know. I mean, the only time he was out of my sight was in the shed. Maybe he fell in there or something. Or maybe he got too hot outside and going into the air conditioning caused him to pass out and go into a seizure."

When they got to St. Joseph Memorial Hospital's emergency room, Beth ran in with Christopher, yelling, crying, "We need help." It was about 12:45 P.M.

Michael Treece was the emergency room physician that day. He took one look at Christopher and knew they had a very sick child on their hands. Christopher was comatose. One side of his body was "stiff as a board, decerebrate. One side was having seizure-like activity." He called Dr. Janet Robinson for assistance; when she arrived at the emergency room, she, too, immediately recognized the severity of the situation. In decerebrate posturing, "the jaw is clenched very tightly, the neck is sort of retracted inward, the arms are extended and rotated to the inside, and so are the legs." Decerebrate posturing means that significant levels of the brain are not functioning because of some sort of severe brain damage. In addition, Treece checked Christopher's eyes and found "multiple areas of retinal hemorrhaging." The heart rate of a normal child is between 110 and 120 beats per minute; Christopher's heart rate was between 60 and 70, indicating that something was impeding his beating heart.

Bewildered by the incongruity between Gary's story and the injuries presented, the staff struggled to ascertain just what was going on with Christopher. "The history I obtained was not consistent with what I saw," Treece would testify later, the terse comment underlining the horror of what was before them. They started Christopher on oxygen, began an IV, intubated him, took a history, and ordered a CT scan and blood tests.

Although Gary hung back, Beth tried to stay with Christopher as long as possible, until it seemed she was in the way of the medical personnel. She and Gary took turns trying to call people, and Beth queried the medical staff rushing in and out of the treatment room. She buttonholed Treece.

"When is he gonna wake up? What's wrong? How long is he gonna be like this?"

At the time, Beth thought Treece was very rude, because he simply threw up his arms, threw off her question, and walked away saying, "I can't tell you anything." Later, she understood exactly why he was so agitated.

Rhonda got back to the trailer around one o'clock and almost immediately thought something was funny. Normally the gentle pit bull was left inside and the mean pit bull was chained up outside, but when she got home, Bonnie was on a chain outdoors and Hooch was inside. She called Beth's and got no answer, and then, thinking that maybe Beth and Gary had the little boys together as they'd planned, she waited about twenty minutes before phoning again. She also thought it was odd that one of Christopher's outfits was soaking in the bathtub. It wasn't the outfit she'd clothed him in that morning. And a small amount of something that looked like barbecue sauce was splattered on the kitchen floor.

When Kevin Lockhart walked into the ER area, he flagged down Dr. Treece, who had been the Lockhart family physician for years.

"Hey, Doc, have you looked at that little baby in there?"

"How is that baby related to you?"

"That's my grandbaby," Kevin replied, still trying to get oriented and not knowing what had transpired. Treece turned white.

"What happened to him?" Treece asked. His voice was not polite. "This baby's been hit before he got here."

"I don't know," Kevin responded, "but I'm going to find out."

Kevin marched to the pastoral care room where Gary was sitting. "I want to know right now what happened to that baby," he said. But all he heard was the story that was becoming a litany. And Gary never did look Kevin in the eye, "just once in a while just glancing by when he was going from the corner to the floor or something."

When Rhonda tried calling again, Gary was on the other end of the line. Apparently he'd finished dialing just as she picked up the phone. He was screaming and crying, so she had trouble making out what he was saying.

"It's Christopher," he finally blurted out.

"What happened? Is he hurt bad?" she asked. But Gary couldn't seem to explain, so he put Dr. Robinson on the phone.

"What is going on?" Rhonda demanded.

"It's bad," Robinson said. "There is blood between the lining of his brain and his skull. You need to get to the hospital right now."

"Oh my God, what could have happened that he would have bleeding in the brain? He was fine this morning, he took a bath with me," she screamed.

Sobbing, nearly hysterical, Rhonda launched herself into Gary's truck and drove like mad, sliding recklessly around the curves of the gravel road. Pictures of Christopher whirled through her head as she flattened the accelerator on the floor — Christopher riding on the vacuum cleaner; Christopher cuddling with her on the couch while they watched TV; Christopher waving good-bye. What in God's name could have happened? Maybe there was something about his being premature, something they hadn't suspected that had ambushed them like this. Leaving the truck running outside the ER, Rhonda raced inside, Christopher's name bursting from her throat as she crashed through the doors.

Christopher was having the CT scan, and someone finally made her realize she'd have to wait to see him. She tried to make some phone calls, but her hands were shaking so much, and she couldn't seem to remember to dial "9" to get an outside line, so she sat, helpless, cursing, until one of the nurses helped her dial. As she waited for Christopher to come out, Beth and Gary joined her, crying. Gary kept saying, "Rhonda, I'm so sorry, I'm so sorry, you know."

Rhonda hadn't been able to locate Joyce yet, but Beth had contacted Chuck, who was still trying to find Debbie, Ruth, and Charlie. Then Christopher came out of the CT scan. Rhonda rushed to his side, talking to him, hoping her voice would get through to him. She thought he kept trying to open his eyes, but he couldn't, and the seizures kept coming, his once round, cuddly body now stiff and helpless before the relentless constrictions. Crouching by the bed, she whispered in his ear, Mommy things, silly things, anything to make him relax, to let him know she was there. She could hardly talk through her tears. Would these be the last words he would hear?

The CT scan showed a large subdural hematoma, bleeding into the inside of the skull. The brain was swollen, and the radiologist, Dr. Steve Walden, thought he detected left frontal, nondepressed skull fractures. His voice echoed down the hall, "Get this kid out of here, he's seriously injured, get him out of here now." St. Joseph's has no neurosurgeon on staff, and Treece and Robinson and Walden now knew Christopher needed more help than they could give him. Quickly, the staff began making preparations to airlift Christopher to St. Louis Children's Hospital.

Chuck got the same story from Gary that everyone else had heard — playing outside, whiny, drink of water, mysterious collapse. But when he finally got a look at Christopher in the ER, he was suspicious. Christopher was much too clean for a child who had been playing outside. "I know my boy like the back of my hand, and if you walk him outside for ten seconds, he is dirty. He just gets into everything, you know? He was spotless—his hands were clean, and there was no dirt under the fingernails or anything." Why had Christopher been cleaned up? Or had he never been outside at all?

Debbie, who'd had the day off, had just walked in from shopping at Wal-Mart when Chuck reached her. She left immediately, pausing only to drop her daughter off at a neighbor's. She walked through the ER doors and saw the staff working on Christopher in the trauma room to the left. Tears in her eyes, she nonetheless willed herself to act as the experienced professional that she was, so she didn't try to go in. She knew the staff didn't need help or emotional onlookers. But her glimpse of Christopher was all it took. She thought to herself, "Oh, this child's gone." She prayed for a miracle if that was possible, but she also prayed, "Don't keep him living like this, because it's not a life."

Christopher was given medication to paralyze him so that he wouldn't expend precious life energy convulsing, and he was wheeled out to the helicopter. Rhonda wanted to ride with him, but the aircraft was filled to capacity with medical personnel. So the family went outside, waiting for the lift-off. It was mid-afternoon.

Joyce drove in from Marion, the same grim thought racing through her head over and over: "What did Gary do to that baby?" When she arrived, the family was dispersing to vehicles for the trip to St. Louis. Rhonda was with Gary. She was sobbing, frightened, and Debbie tried to comfort her.

"Let's just get up there and see what's going to happen. We don't know the whole story yet."

Joyce joined the group. "What's going on?" she demanded.

Debbie replied, "It looks pretty serious. It's a head injury of some kind, he's got a subdural hematoma, but nobody seems to know how it

happened. They're suspecting shaken baby, I think. He'll go into neuro-
surgery as soon as they get there."

"Do you know what that means?" Joyce shrieked. She was freak-
ing out.

"I know, I know," said Debbie, one nurse to another. There wasn't
much else to say. Gary apparently had gotten the drift of things, too,
and he didn't like it.

Right after the aircraft took off, Roger Smith—a surgical RN at
St. Joseph's who had just gotten off work—was walking to his car. He
had not participated in the medical intervention of Christopher, but
he was aware that the child was seriously injured. As he approached his
vehicle, he heard loud voices. A tall, dirty, powerful-looking man with
long hair, wearing only cutoffs, a bandanna, and several tattoos, was
yelling at a small group of people. He had acted scared in the hospital.
Now he was angry.

"Yes, I know what it means," he bellowed. "There's no way you're
going to do that to me. I'm not going to put up with taking the blame
for this."

Roger could hear the man's voice over the retreating sound of the
helicopter but few of the responses of the women who were talking
with him. He thought maybe someone was explaining the implications
of Christopher's injuries as they were understood up to this point, but
the more someone would try to calm him, the more agitated the man
became. He wasn't asking questions about Christopher, he was concerned for himself. He was so angry that Roger thought the confrontation could end in physical blows. Obscenities littered the air, the day
given gruesome, distorted form around the distraught family.

"That isn't going to happen to me. You're not going to put that on
me. The baby fell off the porch," Gary yelled, apparently alluding to
an earlier accident.

"But there wasn't any change in him after he fell off the porch that time," Rhonda screamed back, "and that's the only time he hit his head."

"I never hit him, I never hit him," yelled Gary Gould.

Joyce, Kevin, Robyn, and Buddy piled into one car; Chuck and Debbie picked up Ruth. Charlie went by Martin Foods where Tim was working. Tim broke out in a cold sweat. Every foreboding thought he'd had about Christopher's situation — "the drug use and everything" — was coming true. Unable to find the store manager to tell him he was leaving, Tim left a message with a coworker and walked off the job, joining his father on the terrible drive to St. Louis.

Gary and Rhonda went back to the trailer so Gary could get some clothing. Rhonda grabbed Christopher's good-luck troll baby, which Ruth had bought him when he was born, some clean clothing, diapers, and pacifiers. After gassing up, they followed the path of the rest of the family. They drove in alternating silence and tears, Rhonda crying and Gary breaking the silence to try to explain, saying, "I'm sorry, Rhonda, I'm so sorry, you know." And Rhonda asked him "five times a minute" to tell her again what had happened, desperately hoping to bring a moment of sanity into the picture. But Gary, crying, just repeated what was becoming the story. They were playing outside, squirting with the hose and washing the patio. Christopher seemed like he was hot, so they went inside to get a drink.

"I don't understand if he'd been playing in the water how he could look like he was hot."

"So I took him into the trailer to change his pants, and he was right behind me as I walked into the kitchen. And then his knees buckled and he fell on the floor on his face. I picked him up and turned him over to get him to come to and he kept trying to open his eyes, and he called for Mama, but one eye went this way and one eye went that way. It seemed like he was trying to open his eyes, but he couldn't. Rhonda, it was the worst thing."

"What in God's name could make his eyes go that way?" she cried. "Tell me again, exactly what happened."

And Gary would tell it again. And then he'd lapse into tears, "scared crying."

When Christopher arrived at Children's Hospital, the attending physician, Dr. Barry Markovitz, and the pediatric neurosurgeon, Dr. Bruce Kaufman, already knew they were dealing with an "extremely critical" closed head injury. During the transport, Christopher had begun to have an increase in his blood pressure and a decrease in his pulse. His pupils were fixed and not responsive to light. They reviewed the CT scan and, based upon that and other information, decided to place a monitor to measure the pressure inside the head and help treat the swelling.Because he had a small rim of subdural fluid outside of the brain, they wanted to drain that fluid through a small hole to relieve the pressure at the same time. Just beneath the bone of the skull is the dura, the tough covering of the brain, and underneath the dura was fluid, hence the term "subdural." Some of the fluid unnaturally collected there was a layer of blood (hematoma) "over the entire left hemisphere of the brain, and swelling primarily on that side." They were, in other words, going to put two holes in Christopher's head to monitor the swelling and relieve the intercranial pressure from the swelling and the hematoma. Kaufman placed a burr hole about the "size of a nickel or a quarter to open up through the bone and covering and evacuate the fluid and blood, and then through a very small incision just in front of that, insert a pressure monitor."

After opening the covering of the brain, they found the dura "very tense," and after opening that, according to Kaufman, "we literally got a gush of bloody fluid from above the surface of the brain, and then the fragile brain itself started to come through the hole," so powerful was the pressure within the immovable walls of the skull. Normally, the dura is "pretty loose; normally the fluid beneath the dura is colorless." There was no evidence of old blood clots. The bloody fluid was fresh.

And once they inserted the pressure monitor, they got a reading on the intercranial pressure: it was sixty millimeters of mercury. Normal intercranial pressure is somewhere in the neighborhood of ten to twelve millimeters of mercury. In layperson's terms, Christopher's intercranial pressure was "very elevated, abnormal, four to six times the amount it should be, caused by the swelling of the brain." Clearly, the toddler was suffering from a severe closed head injury. The cause, however, was yet to be determined.

Joyce, Kevin, Robyn, and Buddy were the first to arrive at St. Louis Children's Hospital. They found out that Christopher had gotten out of surgery and was being taken to intensive care. As they waited at the elevator, the doors opened. A patient was being backed out of the elevator. First they saw a six-inch tube coming out the elevator door; then they saw that the tube was attached to Christopher's head.

"I believe we knew," says Joyce, not needing to finish the sentence. None of them could move for a moment, just staring at that fragile head with its downy golden fuzz of hair and the tube sticking out.

Debbie, Chuck, and Ruth and Charlie and Tim all arrived about the same time. They filed quietly into the ICU.

"He's over there," said Charlie.

"That's not Christopher," whispered Debbie.

"Yes it is," Charlie insisted, struggling to keep his voice steady. Christopher didn't look like Christopher anymore. Even though he'd been intubated and had IVs at St. Joseph's, his eyes were closed and he still looked like himself, like he was sleeping. Now his eyes were swollen, although not closed. One eye was open more than the other. Half his head was shaved, and his remaining hair was all messed up from the bandages. They were advised to talk to him because he could hear them, so Ruth bent close to his head to whisper a song. When she started to sing "Itsy-Bitsy Spider," his whole body trembled, and she felt sure that he knew Maw Maw was there. Whenever the staff let her, she was by his bedside, singing, whispering words of hope, waiting.

Early that evening, Dr. Bruce Kaufman summoned the two families into the hallway, near the same elevators where Joyce and her family had first glimpsed Christopher's wounded head. There was nothing reassuring about his manner. He did not say, "I have bad news to tell you." He did not say, "I've got sad news to tell you." "He was pissed off," says Joyce.

"Let me tell you about the extent of damage Christopher has sustained," he began abruptly. And then he laid it out. Christopher was severely brain damaged. He was barely living on life support systems and brain stem function, the higher functions of the brain having been destroyed by the swelling and bleeding. He could not breathe on his own. If he were to regain consciousness, which was unlikely, he would be severely visually impaired, if not blind, having suffered severe retinal damage.

"Is this the result of a fall he had a month ago?" asked Gary, who was standing on the margin of the transfixed group.

"This is not the result of a fall a month ago, or even a week ago. This baby is suffering from severe closed head injury that happened, to the best we can determine, within hours of our seeing him," replied Kaufman. "The combination of brain swelling, the acute blood on top of the brain, and the finding of retinal hemorrhages in conjunction with the other findings indicate nonaccidental trauma."

To the families, his words were accusatory as he looked at them, his eyes searching the entire group, person by person.

"My concern has to be for my patient," he continued. "I'm not accusing anyone here, but these injuries are not an accident, and surely someone out there knows what happened to this baby."

"It was more than we could bear to hear, I think," says Joyce. She watched as Gary turned away, the rest of the group tracking every word Kaufman uttered.

Thus commenced the nightmarish hours of uncertainty as the rest of the family arrived, establishing Attig and Carter/Lockhart outposts in the ICU and awaiting the results of further postsurgical testing, which would include an examination by pediatric ophthalmologist Dr. Gregory Lueder. The hours of hospital time, endless in the false light of eternal day, were remembered in fragmented images, slivers of hallway conversations, emotional scuffles, nervous laughter, pacing, posturing, silence, tears.

The Department of Child and Family Services caseworker was suspicious of Rhonda, who was too distraught to remember what was asked or what she answered. From her position on the end of a gurney in the hall, Ruth heard Gary suggest to Rhonda and Chuck that "this had to be the result of one of the falls Christopher took," referring to any one of four falls he'd sustained since early June: from a chair, against a sharp table, down Joyce's basement stairs, and onto a concrete porch. "There's probably a blood clot in there that moved and, you know, kept oxygen from getting to the brain and everything, and that's why he keeled over like that," Gary offered. Ruth puzzled over this explanation, because this moving blood clot theory sounded to her much like what she'd been told was the cause of her stroke, and no one seemed to think that Christopher had suffered a stroke.

Later, Gary suggested to Joyce that maybe Christopher had been bitten by a snake when he was in the storage shed, a possibility that didn't strike Joyce as too likely because there aren't that many poisonous snakes in southern Illinois "known to cause retinal detachment." In fact, Gary seemed to be working his companions steadily, at least those he felt would give him a hearing. But when he wasn't hanging around acting concerned, he was acting like "he didn't care, like he just wanted to, you know, just get out of there or something. He would sit down against the wall and put his head down. Then he would, like, look up to see if anybody was noticing him. Like he was doing it on purpose," says Tim Attig bitterly.

While Tim was observing Gary with hostile eyes, Chuck was floating anxiously back and forth between his family and Rhonda's, not sure where he belonged, by virtue of his former marriage, by virtue of friendship. Since he'd been prospected for the Phantoms, he and Gary and Terry Hickam had become pals. They partied together a lot. Now, while Rhonda was faced with the possibility that her lover had harmed her child, Chuck was faced with the possibility that his "club" sponsor and friend had harmed his child.

But while Chuck didn't know what to think, others found certainty relatively quickly. Tim wasn't the only person who was suspicious of Gary; Kevin Lockhart had been letting loose remarks, and Ruth wasn't being shy in expressing her opinion that Gary was responsible for Christopher's injuries.

"Mom," said Chuck, "you're starting all kinds of hell, and we can't have that kind of turmoil up here. It's hard enough as it is. You better apologize to Gary for what you've been saying."

Ruth looked at him in disbelief. "I can't apologize to him. These are my feelings. I think he's hurt Christopher. If he didn't, just how do you think this happened?"

Chuck just stared at her, refusing the possibility. "You have to."

So Ruth got up and walked into the waiting area where Rhonda and Gary were "laughing and having a good time," and she said, "I'm sorry if I've said anything that has upset you."

Gary never looked at her. He turned his head the other way, waved his hand nonchalantly, and said, "Ah, that's okay. I know everybody's under a lot of stress." Later, he and Chuck sacked out in the waiting room.

Shortly after midnight, Dr. Kaufman returned. He was terse and no more friendly than the first time. After further observation and testing, Christopher had been diagnosed. He was suffering from Shaken Baby Syndrome. There was little hope for recovery. Now there was nothing to do but keep waiting for the change that would release them for the next terrible act.

Ruth and Kevin had some opinions about how to best spend the time, agreeing that if someone was man enough to go after Gary, it would be a great help to society. Tim Attig was ready to do so, having come to the hospital armed and ready. "I just felt something bad had happened and it wasn't an accident, and I would have just as soon killed him right then and there," he says flatly.

Joyce was horrified at the vigilante talk. "I don't like lynch mobs," she says, "and I could not see doing this to Gary without knowing he was guilty for sure." It may have been Tim's gun, but Joyce knew Chuck's temper the best, and she was worried he would do something rash.

"Chuck," she said, "you need to stay calm. Be rational and let the police and the authorities take care of it. It's out of our hands now. We have our own things to deal with." Tim doesn't remember who talked him out of killing Gary, but someone, maybe Ruth, maybe Chuck, "who always tries to look out for me," persuaded him to take his gun back out of the hospital.

It was nearly 3:00 A.M., and Joyce and Rhonda hustled Gary outside. For Rhonda's protection, Joyce wanted to be a witness if they had words. Then, she did the talking.

"I think you'd better go on home," Joyce advised. "Things are getting pretty hot-tempered in there, and the evidence is really stacking up against you."

"But it could have been a fall, or maybe Chuck did it while Christopher was with him in July," Gary protested.

"That's not what the doctors are saying, Gary. They're saying it happened recently, that the last person who had Christopher when he was well is the person who did it."

"Well, what's gonna happen next?"

"Christopher's not going to make it," she said, letting her words sink in. "The police will want to talk to you tomorrow, and we'll just have to wait and see what happens."

"If he dies, I'm out of here. I'm going to Florida and you'll never see me again."

"That won't do, Gary. You need to be here and answer questions. It'll be much worse for you if you run."

"But what's gonna happen when those doctors say I did it and I say I didn't?" he asked.

"If it comes down to that, they're going to believe the medical experts," she replied.

"But," he persisted, "if I say I didn't do it, it will be my word against theirs no matter what, right?"

What could she say? That was about the size of it, but what did it mean that this was the way Gary was responding to the situation? He didn't seem concerned at all for the toddler who lay dying in the hospital behind them. In fact, she couldn't recall him saying much of anything about Christopher the entire, dreadful night except to make up explanations for the injury. She didn't want to believe this of him, for Rhonda's sake, if nothing else.

"Yeah, well, I'm out of here," he said. "I've got some business to take care of anyway."

"Oh yeah," she thought, watching him walk off to his truck, "those marijuana plants by the back door. Well, he and Rhonda have enough going on already, let him get rid of them. They don't need any more trouble."

By the time Lieutenant Michael Teas arrived to inspect the crime scene, the trailer had been tidied, the four-wheeler was in the shed, and the back door was innocent of illegal weed.

By 4:00 P.M. the next day, August 4, Christopher's clinical condition had deteriorated. His intercranial pressure remained high, unresponsive to treatment, while his blood pressure fell below the intercranial pressure. There were no anesthetics or medications that could be causing these results; the cause was slow brain death. For a second time, Kaufman noted lack of brain stem reflexes consistent with brain death: no response to facial pain, no gag reflex, no response to ice water in the ear, no oculocephalic reflexes, no pupillary reflexes, and no effort at spontaneous respiration. Kaufman relayed this information to the family and broached the subject of organ donation.

Still trying to absorb the fact of her son's impending death, Rhonda was resistant to organ donation at first, but Chuck convinced her of the rightness of the idea. Together, they went out and bought Christopher a red baseball cap to cover the holes in his head. It said "Champ." Then each family member came in to hold him one last time and say goodbye in a memorial photograph. Heads bent low over the dying child, or tear-blinded faces turned toward the camera in mute witness of what was happening, they all looked the same, unrecognizable, conjoined in the ravages of grief.

Christopher looked the same in each photograph, too. His eyes were swollen shut, his face distorted beyond recognition. The lusty, fat-cheeked toddler, the happy boy with the mischievous brown eyes who loved to smell marigolds and mess with the dog water and dance around the house in his big, floppy hat and eat spaghetti with his daddy and ride in Gary's truck and help Paw Paw in the workshop and roll around the floor with his uncle Tim and aggravate his aunt Robyn and ride on Katie and play peekaboo in Ruth's front curtains and dance the Hokey Pokey and take naps on his uncle Buddy and roughhouse with Joyce and eat corn on the cob—that unique, one of a kind Christopher—was gone. He came into the world miraculously, sustained by tubes and machines as a fragile newborn. He left the world unnaturally, sustained by tubes and machines, blinded, brain damaged, unable to hold up his head or his limbs, a thirty-five-pound newborn into death. Swaddled in blankets, cradled in each set of arms, he was tiny once again.

Christopher Michael Attig was pronounced dead at 7:42 P.M., August 4, 1994.

6

Living with the Enemy

I don't know anybody who could be around him for five minutes that he couldn't make smile. He's probably up there in heaven, making everybody laugh and smile so.

Chuck may have been ambivalent at first, but once he heard Kaufman, he found certainty. At dawn on Thursday morning, he called Debbie, who had returned home late Wednesday night. "Gary killed my baby," he said, weeping. "He shook my baby to death."

Christopher was buried with his good-luck troll baby, wearing a Harley hat and a Harley shirt. At Rhonda and Chuck's request, Ruth went to the Harley store in Marion to get him the shirt, but she was unable to decide which one to get. Noting the store's "no return" policy, she told the store manager the circumstances and asked if she could take two shirts and show them to Chuck and Rhonda and return the one they didn't want. He gave her both shirts.

And so the mischievous, fat-cheeked little boy who'd barely begun to talk was laid to rest in a remote rural cemetery. The stone is heart-shaped with a lamb carved on the front. Ruth keeps one side of the grave decorated with wind socks and flowers and small figures and plaques that recognize the changing of seasons. His Sesame Street figures line the front of the stone, and Rhonda hangs wind chimes on the other side.

Usually burial is a significant, if preliminary, form of closure for the grieving process — except for families of murdered children. For them, closure is always deferred and elusive. Their journey through the justice system is just beginning, and the legal process that intervenes in the natural course of grieving is rarely a healing procedure. This is not a death that brings families closer together; one does not expect great epiphanies from such senseless suffering and loss. The two families squared off and backed off and waited, and in the interim between Christopher's death and the beginning of the trial, each did their best to cope with the relentless pain.

None of the Attigs had any doubt as to what happened to Christopher, but things were not so clear-cut in the Carter/Lockhart household. Joyce had considered Gary a family member, perhaps a future son-in-law. Now she was considering whether he had killed her grandson. "I hate to think the worst of people," she says. "I was pretty sure that Gary had done this, but there was the possibility and a hope that maybe he hadn't. What if the autopsy showed something else from one of those falls? [I thought,] maybe Gary is innocent, and until I hear differently that's how I'm going to take it."

Robyn felt the same way. "I tried to put my faith in Gary because he had never given me any reason to doubt him."

As for Rhonda, she had the most difficult time absorbing the betrayal. "On August 4 I lost my son, I lost the man I loved, I lost my home, my dog, I mean just my whole life, and so it was like I had to hold onto whatever I could hold onto, even if it was the bad part." In the days after Christopher's death, she stuck by Gary, as did most of the Carter/Lockhart household. Gary and Rhonda didn't want to live at the trailer, so Robyn offered to share her living space with them. Joyce agreed, because "at that time I was willing to do anything at all that would comfort Rhonda." The basement of the Lockhart house has a full kitchen and functioning bathroom, and Robyn had fixed it up as a small apartment. And so for five weeks, Gary lived in the Lockhart basement with Rhonda and Robyn. Rhonda, who was seriously depressed, stayed below, and if Joyce wanted to see her, she had to visit her own basement, where Rhonda insisted on keeping the lights off.

So many little things happened in those weeks that made Rhonda suspicious. She was leery of Gary, sometimes watching him, waiting for a look or a word that would tell her. At other times, she could hardly bear to look at him, and when he touched her, she shrank away. She didn't want to sleep with him. She lost so much weight she was prescribed medication to restore her appetite.

At first, Gary was eager to normalize. Robyn found him curiously friendly with her, chatting with her about her friends and activities in a way he'd never done before. But if Christopher's name came up, he grew cold, and soon he'd find an excuse to leave. Joyce heard him talk expansively about future plans. Although he hadn't paid child support for his own daughter for many months and had been unemployed for as long, he seemed to have the capital to make a substantial cash payment on a new car, or maybe he'd get a motorcycle, he hadn't decided. But he definitely wanted to go somewhere. Rhonda, however, only traveled as far as Christopher's room, to sit amidst his toys. Not once did Gary express sorrow or sympathy or even gratitude for their willingness to presume him innocent until proven guilty. Instead, he got angry with the grieving family around him, and as the weeks wore on, the Carter/Lockhart household saw less and less of him.

Gary not only seemed to avoid contact with the family that was sheltering him, he also became angry when Rhonda would speak of Christopher or talk about what had happened.

"What's wrong with you?" he asked Rhonda. "Why can't you just leave it alone?"

"Wrong with me? You won't even look at his things or go into his room. Why won't you talk about Christopher, Gary?"

"Because it's the worst thing that's happened to me in my life, and I don't like talking about it."

He tried to resume their nightlife of partying, but Rhonda just "couldn't get with it." If people asked her about Christopher, she'd cry, and then Gary would get mad. He said his anger was on her behalf; he didn't want to hear talk about Christopher because it upset her. Gary thought if she put away Christopher's pictures and got rid of his toys she wouldn't be sad, and he did his part by setting an example. He avoided all reference to Christopher. Sometimes in the night, though, Rhonda would crawl to the end of the bed as though Christopher's crib was still there and, talking in her sleep, try to cover him up. She would wake up bent over the end of the bed, stunned by the slow run of tears into the empty darkness. And sometimes in the night, Rhonda would wake up and stare at the silent hulk next to her, thinking about killing him while he was sleeping, wondering how you could do that to a baby you loved.

"I know Gary loved Christopher," says Joyce. "I saw them interact in positive ways. And Christopher loved Gary. When Gary would walk into a room, Christopher would light up, and Christopher tried to spit and walk the way Gary did." Joyce thought that maybe by living with Rhonda and Robyn, Gary got some comfort. Then again, she thought that maybe he was using them as cover, so "people wouldn't think he had done it." Kevin, on the other hand, was firmly opposed to Gary living with them, but he couldn't seem to get through to Joyce or Robyn, who had closed ranks in protection of Rhonda. Kevin registered his protest by moving out of the house for a week, hoping to get some perspective. Gary finally persuaded Rhonda to come out from underground, and they took a Labor Day trip with friends to Maryland.

Meanwhile, Ruth Attig was calling prosecutor Michael Wepsiec's office almost daily. Why hadn't they arrested Gary Gould? It humiliated her, infuriated her that Gary was hanging around town free and easy when the answer to Christopher's death seemed so obvious. Then on September 8, the autopsy report arrived, strengthening Ruth's conviction that something should be done immediately. According to Dr. Michael Graham, St. Louis County Medical Examiner, Christopher Attig died as the result of a closed head injury, marked by "diffuse axonal injury, subdural hematoma, bilateral retinal hemorrhages and right retinoschisis, subarachnoid hemorrhage and brain death." The manner of death? "Homicide." And yes, he'd had a mild ear infection. But for Michael Wepsiec, Shaken Baby Syndrome was new territory, and he wanted to make sure he understood all the medical dimensions of the case before making an arrest. The investigators were still interviewing witnesses, and both Lieutenant Teas and the DCFS caseworker had a question about the identity of Christopher's killer — was it Gary Gould or Rhonda Carter? Charging someone with first degree murder or involuntary manslaughter is a serious matter, because, in Wepsiec's words, "despite all the platitudes we have about presumption of innocence, once you charge somebody, they are believed to have committed the crime in the eye of the public." He didn't want to make a mistake that could have serious consequences for everyone involved.

Rhonda came to the police station to read the autopsy report, and "I just lost it. I didn't know what to do. Like here I was, all alone. I used to hang onto Gary or my little sister whenever I had a bad problem, and nobody was there." She called Joyce, who immediately walked off the job and picked up her distraught daughter. They drove around for hours, as Rhonda struggled to confront the final implications of the report.

"Mom, he did it, he did it, oh God, he did it," she cried over and over again. "I thought we'd get married one day," she gasped, "what was I thinking? I must have been in never-never land. Oh God, he did it. Mom, I've been living with my son's killer. Oh my God, oh my God."

In one way, this was a turning point for Rhonda. Two days later, she told Gary about the autopsy report, and he left the Carter/Lockhart household. This apparently wasn't a great hardship for him. After evicting Rhonda from the trailer — which she hadn't lived in for at least a month — he soon moved in with his new girlfriend, whom he'd been seeing while he was with Rhonda. But Rhonda's loyalty to him continued to lead her into confusing and contradictory pathways, which in turn made it difficult for Wepsiec to arrive at a clear determination of who to charge with the crime.

In late September, Rhonda flunked her polygraph test, although a day later she called to arrange for an interview in which she wanted to explain and tell the truth. She confessed to lying on some questions to protect Gary, who had warned her not to say anything about drugs, guns, or the motorcycle club. Upon the advice of her counselor, she wrote several letters to Gary expressing her feelings, and she sought an opportunity to read her letter to him. This gave her a reason to call him. She usually tried contacting him through Beth, who had the impression that Rhonda still had strong feelings for Gary. Apparently, Rhonda continued to see him off and on through that fall, and Gary pressured her to get back together with him. Gary had become the most powerful, destructive drug of all.

Although Gary had never hurt her like Chuck had, Rhonda was afraid of Gary. He'd pushed her around some, and there was always the threat of the biker club backing up his orders. After she leveled with the police about the drug and gun activity at the trailer, she began getting threats from his friends. Anonymous phone calls promised that she and her family could expect retaliation. She was bartending one afternoon when several of Gary's friends from the club came in and gathered in front of her at the bar.

"I heard you mentioned my name to the police," said a guy named Cam. He'd always been nice to her, but now he didn't look very happy.

"Your name may have been mentioned. But only if it was something that Gary has done that may have included you. But nothing that you've actually done." She stopped working and stared at them. She was scared, although it was late in the afternoon and there were people around.

"Yeah, well, that's not what I heard," someone else growled.

"What we hear is you set him up."

"Well, I didn't. Gary's in trouble because he got hisself there. Maybe you shouldn't be judging me until you have all the info, you know? Even his mother knows he did it. Yeah. And Chuck's family is all bent out because I still talked to him, and now you guys are on my case because I won't talk to him. Which way am I supposed to go?"

"Yeah, maybe we ought to think of a way you'll think twice before you narc again."

"My child is dead," Rhonda cried back at them, her voice breaking. "What else do you want from me?" Then she went ballistic, crying, kicking the back of the bar, pounding on the bar top. "Yeah, right, go ahead, you all are so big and bad. But my baby is dead. Dead, do you get it? So nothing is going to stop me from testifying, nothing is going to stop me from telling the truth. So you take your choice. Either I'm going in there or you're going to kill me. It's not about what I'm going through, or Gary, or anyone else, it's about Christopher." The bar was silent for a minute as the ragged, wild sound of her voice echoed and stopped. Several people shuffled nervously and backed away, leaving only Cam in front of her.

"I'm sorry," he mumbled. "I didn't realize."

"I'm sorry for taking it out on you," she responded. "But you can't come in here with this attitude when you were supposed to be my friend, too. If this is how you do me, who cares if I told on you? Who cares about Gary? He doesn't deserve to get run over by a Mack truck, but he killed a baby. We're talking about Christopher being dead. That never changes. What about that little baby who trusted Gary, huh?" Silently, he embraced her over the counter and then left.

Because Rhonda had been one of the last to be with Christopher before he was fatally assaulted and because of her performance on behalf of Gary, Wepsiec had considered charging her, but his ongoing fact-finding about SBS and his consultations with Dr. Bruce Kaufman brought him clarity, and he swung his suspicions squarely back upon

Gary Gould. Gary had refused to take a polygraph test but had otherwise cooperated with the process. He spoke melodramatically to Rhonda of "going down alone" and "taking the rap alone," but when Beth spoke up to him, he wasn't acting, he was angry.

"One of you guys knows what happened to Christopher," she said. "You or Rhonda were the only ones with him. I can't imagine either one of you living the rest of your life knowing that you did something to hurt Christopher." At first, he didn't comment.

"Somebody needs to speak up," she persisted.

"I'm tired of talking about it," he answered. "I'm sick of everybody bringing it up all the time. I talked to my lawyer and he said there's nothing to worry about anyway because there wasn't enough evidence and it would probably all be dropped. It's all circumstantial, and it's hard to prove anything like that in court."

Beth thought it likely he had done something to Christopher, gotten scared, and now couldn't bring himself to admit it. But she was never able to persuade him to clear his conscience. Perhaps he was too willing to believe his lawyer and was just arrogant enough to think he could beat the system, so that even when he was arrested on October 19, 1994, his story was consistent. He was charged with two counts of first degree murder and one count of involuntary manslaughter.

Once bail was reduced from $750,000 to $50,000, he made bail and was back out in late November. Perhaps being free again made him reckless. Perhaps he was so confident he could beat the system that he never thought twice about allegedly threatening and raping Rhonda on Christmas Eve. Perhaps he was scared. Perhaps he just wasn't very bright.

Because Joyce had been working long hours, Kevin was on the road, and Buddy was staying with relatives, Rhonda had temporarily moved in with her aunt. She couldn't bear being alone. It was December 24, in the early afternoon. Rhonda was getting dressed, expecting to hear from Chuck. They were going together to put a candle on Christopher's grave. So, when she answered the door wearing a knee-length flannel shirt and panties, she was caught off-guard by Gary. He was wearing a black t-shirt, green flannel shirt, jeans, Harley boots — and an attitude. He pushed his way through the door.

"I'm having a bad day," she said. "Leave me alone." She walked into the bedroom to continue dressing. He followed her.

"I want to know what you've been saying to the police," he said, grabbing her by the arm. She jerked away.

"Quit it. I've got to get ready for work."

"I hear you've been seeing Ricky O'Donnell. I don't want you screwing around with my friends, got it?"

"That's none of your business," she replied. "I don't belong to you, remember? Now would you just leave?" She headed for the bedroom door.

He grabbed her, threw her on the bed, and sat on top of her. He drew his knife and put it to her eye, then her throat. She lay there frozen, feeling the cool blade against her skin.

"I'll slice your fuckin' throat, bitch," he growled. Abruptly, he changed tone. "Baby, I love you," he crooned. "I really miss you." As she sobbed quietly, he began pacing. She'd never seen him like this before, a monster one minute, the man she loved the next.

"What is it with you, Gary?" she quavered, not moving.

Still holding the knife, he leaned over the bed again and wiped the tears off her face. Slowly, deliberately, he lowered the knife. More pacing. To her surprise, he answered.

"I don't know. It's like I have two doors in my head. There's an evil side and a good side. I used to be able to go back and forth; the doors were always open. Like if I get on the bad side, it's okay, because I could always come back to the good side. But now the door's closed. It's like I'm stuck, you know?"

"Gary," she began hesitantly, "it's not too late."

But the Gary she knew was gone again. The door was shut. He turned and raised the knife to her again.

"I know the feds are following me. They are all over my ass, everywhere I go. You're the reason I'm going to jail."

"No, I'm not. You're going to jail because of your actions, not my actions. I haven't done anything. Now get out of here."

"If you've narced on me, you'd better fix it. I hear you talked a lot. I'm watching you. I know everything—where you work, who you're seeing. You can't get away with nothing, baby, understand?"

Confused, angry, she turned and cried out at him, "Well, what was I supposed to do, Gary? I had to tell them. When they asked me a question, I didn't care if it was, you know, the most awful thing in the world about myself, I have to tell them the truth. They're investigating my child's death, or have you forgotten that? Do you suppose you could think about that little nineteen-month-old baby who's six feet under right now who never even got to live his life?"

She rolled off the bed and walked toward the dresser.

"I still love you," he said, moving toward her.

"Things aren't the way they used to be," she said flatly.

But as if to demonstrate otherwise, he grabbed at her, pulling at her clothing, trying to undress her. Roughly, he thrust his hands into her underwear.

"Stop it," she fumed, twisting away from him. "You're hurting me." They stumbled together, falling across the bed. As they were struggling, the phone rang. From the other end of the trailer Rhonda heard her nephew calling to her. They both stopped moving, solidified in the grotesque posture of rape.

"Chuck's on the phone for you."

"What does he want?" asked Gary. She picked up the extension. On the other end, Chuck heard her voice. They exchanged greetings, and

Chuck began to ask about their meeting at the cemetery. But suddenly her voice became muffled and then the line went dead.

Gary finished what he'd started with a two-minute intercourse. Rhonda rolled over and faced the wall, not even bothering to fix her clothing, while Gary got dressed and then moved to the bedroom window to admire his Grand Prix.

"Hey, get up and look at my new car."

"I don't care about the car," she muttered. Her sullenness couldn't dampen his newly acquired enthusiasm.

"We could go anywhere in the U.S. in that car," he said. "Or we could sell it and get something different, and it could be just like it used to be." She didn't answer.

"Don't you say nothing to nobody," he warned. "I want to see you again. Is it okay if I come back?" More silence.

Then she said, "I don't care what you do."

All compassion, he leaned over and kissed her on the forehead and said, "I love you, baby." Then he left.

"That Christmas was the worst time of our lives," says Joyce. "We made it through December 7 [what would have been Christopher's second birthday], and then this." Joyce had "spent every dime I could get my hands on to make Christmas better, get them things that they wanted, and spent way too much money, probably $700 to $800 apiece on my children." But when Rhonda came over to her mother's for the gift exchange, Joyce knew right away that something was wrong. They opened some presents, but talk kept returning to Christopher, remembering his miraculous Christmas birth, his first birthday—and then remembering that there was nothing more to remember. The Lockhart family cried together. Then Rhonda took her mother into the bathroom and told her everything that had just transpired with Gary, saying, "Don't say anything to anyone; I don't want Christmas to be ruined for everybody. It's bad enough already."

The Monday after Christmas Day, Chuck took Rhonda out for a

drive, and she confided in him also. He drove her straight to the police station, and with his support, she filed a complaint. A warrant for arrest was issued, citing violation of bail bond, sexual assault, and harassment of a witness. Bail was set by Judge Watt for $250,000. The warrant was served on December 29, and Gary Gould went back to jail to await trial for the murder of Christopher Attig.

7

"He Never Had a Chance
Outside of His Grandparents"

*We had a storybook where Grover goes to the library and the
man tells him, "Shhh." You'd ask Christopher, "What did
the man tell Grover?" and he'd go, "Shhh."*

On March 20, 1995, seventy citizens were gathered for jury selection for the trial of Gary Lynn Gould. The *voir dire* took
two days. "In the twenty-seven years I have been involved,
either as a prosecutor, defense attorney, or judge, I have never seen the
jury selection process in Jackson County that we went through in this
case," commented Judge Watt. What was unusual was the use of questionnaires as a screening device, a procedure never before used in
a Jackson County criminal case. This process of written survey was
added because of the emotionally fraught issues involved. Each juror
filled out a lengthy form designed to reveal our experiences and pre-
dispositions. Examination of each prospective juror during the *voir dire*
was informed by these questionnaires, which were read by Judge Watt
and the prosecution and defense lawyers in the case. The other unusual procedure was the selection of three alternate jurors. Judge Watt
felt that the trial material was so emotionally wrenching, he wanted to
minimize any opportunity for mistrial.

According to the information presented to us by Judge Watt, Gary
Lynn Gould was charged with two counts of first degree murder: that

he shook Christopher Attig, knowing that such action would cause his death; and that he repeatedly shook Christopher Attig, knowing that such action created a strong probability of bodily harm, thereby causing his death. He was also charged with one count of involuntary manslaughter: that he acted in a reckless manner, performing an act likely to cause death or great bodily harm in that he repeatedly shook Christopher Attig, causing a closed head injury that resulted in his death.

The opening procedure had the curious air of both theater and a social event. We all got introduced. Representing the state's attorney and the people of the state of Illinois was Michael Wepsiec, who greeted us and said, "Thank you for coming here today."

Then the defense lawyer and his client presented themselves. "Good morning, ladies and gentlemen. My name is Paul Christenson. It is my duty and pleasure to represent the defendant in this case, Mr. Gary Gould. This is Mr. Gould."

As I mentally fumbled with the word "pleasure"—I found it a strange word for the occasion, although I was hard-pressed to think of an alternative, and how else would the defense lawyer demonstrate his confidence in his client?— Gould stood up. Before us was a tall, well-built young man. His short, dark hair was neatly trimmed, his cream-colored suit bagging at the ankles as though it were not a native garment for him, a costume borrowed from some other man.

"Good morning, ladies and gentleman," he said inclining his head slightly and looking gravely around the room. He looked, I reported to my husband that evening, like he'd been told to act sincere, so he'd put on his sincere face for us all.

Finally, we met the assistant to the defense. As the trial proceeded, it looked to me like it was her job to decorate Gould's left arm, and periodically she would touch him and lean toward him confidingly, her face wreathed in sympathetic curves. I decided that she, too, was part of the theater. She was there to assure the women jurors that Gary was an okay guy. After all, if this tastefully appointed woman could sit right next to him and act like it was a congenial experience, how bad could he be?

A small, feline man with silvering hair curling around his collar, Christenson prowled and insinuated his way through the defense. He worked overtime cultivating the impression that the judge's periodic rulings were prejudicial against the defense, a sort of "poor me" tactic that I supposed was anticipating any appeal and intended to enlist the sympathy of the jury. In fact, the transcript of the pretrial proceedings reveal that Christenson was knowingly pushing the boundaries of pretrial agreements and instructions. Surely this backfired, because he looked much less the martyr than simply incompetent. There were several times when Judge Watt had to tell him how to ask a question so as to overwrite an objection or how to lay a foundation so as to impeach a witness. No setback seemed to temper the exaggerated drama of his presentation, however, and he proved as supple on the courtroom floor as he was with the facts.

In contrast, State's Attorney Michael Wepsiec was low-key and methodical, a man given to occasional sarcasm but not theatrics. Christopher was sick the night of August 2 with an earache? Gary Gould was supposed to be a loving father figure? Well then, why was he out bar-hopping until 2:00 A.M.? "Fine father figure he is! Give me a break," snorted Wepsiec. So physically contained was his presentation that his one memorable gesture during the trial appeared in his closing argument. In a sudden turn away from the jury, he angled toward Gould: "Ladies and gentlemen, you have one and only one verdict to sign, and that is 'We the jury find Gary Gould guilty of first degree murder.'" Like a railroad crossing rail, his arm came up and swung down toward Gould on the words "find Gary Gould guilty." Curiously, for all its awkwardness, the wooden motion carried the passion of his conviction, as the words dropped so bluntly before us.

On the day of jury selection, however, I had no opinion as to Gould's guilt or innocence; I knew nothing about the case, and I was only vaguely aware of Shaken Baby Syndrome. I reminded myself, an insincere man is not necessarily a guilty man. Maybe Gould just naturally has a smart-aleck face; perhaps he is scared. But it didn't help to watch him the next day, as the *voir dire* concluded. Gould lounged in his chair, inspected us all, sometimes seeming to smirk as people answered questions designed to elicit hidden bias. He gave off the unconcerned air of a man who hadn't a care in the world. As we left the courthouse that day, one of the prospective jurors was in tears after the selection process. She thought the defendant should have shown some remorse or seriousness. She thought he looked "smug," "cocky." I had to agree.

The prosecutor's case against Gould depended upon medical evidence from beginning to end. There was no question as to what killed Christopher. He sustained a closed head injury induced by shaking. There was also no question about the time frame within which the fatal injuries were delivered. Because a fatally shaken child becomes symptomatic immediately, the injuries could only have occurred between the time Christopher was last seen alive and well and the time when he was rushed to St. Joseph's hospital. These two facts — the diagnosis and the time frame — were crucial to the prosecution's case.

What Paul Christenson had going for the defense was the consistency of his client's story — the mysterious midmorning collapse — and the absence of witnesses. The only witness was dead. Pretrial motions eliminated material about Gary's prior arrests and drug convictions, his tattoos, and his biker activities, so he did not have to combat problems with character image. But an absence of negative information about his client was not the same as positive input, and Christenson couldn't mount a defense based solely on such evidence. All he could do was cast doubt upon the medical evidence in such a way as to suggest that some other agent could have been responsible. He came close to suggesting that a mysterious stranger could have broken into the trailer on the night of August 2–3 and shaken Christopher while

Rhonda and Gary were sleeping, but his preferred theory was that Rhonda herself had killed her little boy.

Knowing this would likely be a defense strategy, the prosecution made sure that its witnesses stayed away from any evidence that might undercut Rhonda's credibility, and prosecution testimony avoided revealing any inner-family tensions about Rhonda's fitness as a mother. Wepsiec's goal was to carve a straight and narrow path of testimony toward Gary, a pathway cleared and defined to the end by the medical evidence. Even so, although pretrial motions had excluded all evidence about Rhonda's drug use, her disastrous marriage to Chuck, and Chuck's own inglorious arrest record, there was still enough testimony to make it clear that Rhonda was a neglectful custodial mother and Chuck was an absent father.

But convicting Rhonda of being an irresponsible mother wasn't a strong enough defense to save Gary, either. Being rough with your child, as Rhonda sometimes was, didn't make her a killer, unless you wish to indict all parents on the same grounds. Most of us, at one time or another, are guilty of having yanked at a child too hard, and every parent on the jury — and there were at least seven — knew this. To plant a reasonable doubt in the minds of the jury, the defense still had to come to terms with the medical evidence. To make plausible the theory that Rhonda was the guilty party, Paul Christenson created two medical fictions, and then he vibrated between them throughout the trial.

The first medical fiction Christenson produced was what I'll call the "long-term undiagnosed skull fracture." When Christopher was taken to St. Joseph's hospital, the radiologist, Dr. Steve Walden, reported that the CT scan showed evidence of "left frontal nondepressed skull fractures." Seizing upon this reading, Christenson argued that because Christopher had sustained four falls in the months prior to his death, and because no x-ray was taken of any of these falls, the CT scan was, in fact, revealing the cause of Christopher's brain injuries — a long-term undiagnosed skull fracture.

Unfortunately for the defense, the radiologist was wrong in his reading of the CT scan. Dr. Treece testified that "there was a question as to whether or not he had a skull fracture," and Dr. Robinson said she did not see any skull fracture. And, unfortunately for Gould, Christenson hadn't done his homework. This deficit was quickly revealed in his questioning of the St. Louis County medical examiner, Dr. Michael Graham:

Q: Did you see evidence of a left frontal nondepressed skull fracture, sir?

A: There wasn't a skull fracture.

Q: Would you agree with me that a visual examination such as you conducted would not be as accurate as a CT scan?

A: No, just the opposite. The direct examination of the bone [as part of the autopsy] is much more specific than is a CT for demonstrating fractures of the skull.

When Wepsiec returned for the redirect examination, he gave Graham further opportunity to refute Christenson:

Q: Dr. Graham, do you normally perform CT scans when you are doing an autopsy?

A: No.

Q: Doctor, why is direct examination of the skull better than a CT scan for determining whether fractures exist?

A: A CT scan is a sophisticated x-ray technique, but you are still looking at basically shadows or two-dimensional pictures of something. When you are looking at the skull, you have got the bone in your hand and you can look at it, you can move it, and it is just much more accurate.

Undeterred by this blunt correction of his foray into forensic medicine, Christenson returned to the illusive skull fracture in the recross-examination. First, he attempted to tarnish the integrity of Graham's investigation.

> Q: How much time did you take examining this child?
> A: I don't remember.
> Q: How much time did you take examining the head of this child?
> A: I don't remember. I do the case until I feel that I am done. Time is not really an issue in this.

Christenson's retort was both sarcastic and misrepresentative. In exaggerated tones of disbelief, he responded, "This child's skull is an issue in this case and you are telling us you don't remember examining the skull?" Then, brandishing an article from *Pediatrics*, Christenson referred the coroner to a quotation that indicated that a CT scan has "assumed the first line role in the imaging evaluation of the brain injured child." Graham agreed with this statement, pointedly noting that it refers to the use of the CT scan with a *living* child, not a dead child. The CT scan is best at looking inside the skull, not at the skull itself.

"If they [Walden] interpreted a skull fracture," Graham concluded, "then they misinterpreted something on the CT scan."

"Walden made a mistake?" Christenson asked. Then he indulged in a favorite gesture: he stalked toward the jury and inclined his head at the jurors, cuing us to this outrageous suggestion by giving us the significant eye.

"If he says there's a skull fracture, then he made a mistake," replied Graham firmly.

The final damage to the skull fracture theory was the simple fact that Christenson never called the radiologist, a local doctor, to the stand to testify. It seemed clear to me that the reason must be that, knowing you can't argue with the direct examination of the skull conducted during the autopsy, Walden would have had to admit he'd made a mistake. The last thing Christenson wanted was to have the skull fracture repudiated by its creator.

Therefore, he continued his case as though Graham had not corrected Walden's findings and persisted to countenance the possibility of a long-term undiagnosed skull fracture, caused by any one of the undocumented falls Christopher had allegedly sustained. The injury by fall became part of his second medical fiction, "the accumulated fatal injury over time."

That is, Christenson tried to argue that because Christopher had fallen several times, because he had this (nonexistent) skull fracture, because he had an ear infection, because he was whiny and irritable that morning, Gould had been given charge of a fatally injured child. He theorized that perhaps all these symptoms indicated that Christopher had been mildly shaken many times in the preceding months and these multiple shakings collected a fatal force on the morning of August 3, 1994, causing Christopher to collapse mysteriously while in Gould's keeping. This theory allowed him to suggest that Rhonda, not Gary, was responsible for Christopher's death. Perhaps she did it in the night, and then, feeling guilty, took a bath with the baby next morning as a form of postbattery bonding. She left the dying child with Gary, who became the victim in this matter, the unwitting custodian of a brain-injured child.

Knowing nothing about SBS except that it happened, and having no medical knowledge of head injuries in general, I had been open to the possibility that an undetected head injury — perhaps the skull fracture, perhaps a fall more serious than it had seemed — contributed to Christopher's death. But once Graham testified, that possibility was gone. I didn't know about accumulated injury, however. To a lay person, this had some plausibility. But Christenson couldn't get the medical experts to support this theory, either. Not only was there no skull fracture, the four falls Christopher sustained were, medically speaking, "trivial." Like Graham, Dr. Bruce Kaufman, the pediatric neurosurgeon, insisted that he "saw no evidence of any cumulative injuries in Christopher Attig." The only "progressive" injury he suffered was from the "acute injury that we were dealing with." He progressed from coma and "minimal brain function and severe injury . . . to the point where his brain died and he was therefore declared dead." Drs. Graham, Kaufman, Treece, and Gregory Lueder, the pediatric ophthalmologist, all agreed: an injury like Christopher's does not accumulate over time, not from falls, not from prior shakings. As Graham stated firmly, a child with Christopher's injuries "is symptomatic immediately after being lethally shaken. The child may live for an extended period of time, albeit unconscious, but I have never said that the child could be injured twenty-four hours earlier and be normal and then develop symptoms."

As for the subsidiary red herrings — the falls, the earache, lethargy, and whining — the medical experts were equally adamant.

Can an ear infection be confused with SBS?

"No."

What if the child is lethargic?

"A fatally injured child does not simply exhibit lethargy."

Is a blood clot (subdural hematoma) a normal childhood illness?

"No."

Can you get SBS from falling onto a concrete sidewalk? Running into a chair? Could any of his falls have caused these injuries?

"No," said Kaufman and Lueder.

"Children do not receive fatal injuries falling on tables, falling off couches, falling off porches, or tumbling down the stairs," said Dr. Graham. If they did, "we would have hundreds of thousands of children with this condition because [toddlers] fall down each and every day," commented Wepsiec in his closing argument, urging the jury to use their common sense. "[T]here is no evidence of any old injury," Graham said.

Christenson concentrated upon the medical areas most vulnerable to doubt, although the medical testimony revealed that he had little room to maneuver. Unless he was forced by cross-examination of prosecution witnesses, Christenson avoided engaging in any discussion of Christopher's eye injuries, and wisely so. Why? Because to do so would have made transparent the shallowness of the defense. Correspondingly, "[t]he eyes are the windows to the crime," Wepsiec coached the jury.

When Dr. Lueder examined Christopher's eyes, he found "diffuse hemorrhages in the retina," that is, "little spots of bleeding all over the eye . . . too many to count."

"This injury raises suspicions that the child had been shaken?" queried Wepsiec.

"Exactly," responded Lueder. The damage to Christopher's eyes was even more extensive, however. In addition to the profuse swelling in both eyes, the right eye had a retinoschisis cavity, "one of the worst injuries you can get with a shaken baby." What this means is that Christopher's right eye had been split, torn away from the anchoring fibers, creating the schisis cavity, "which is basically not seen in anything else in children except a severe shaking injury," concluded Lueder. The child suffering from such an injury would be "severely" visually impaired; he or she would have "difficulty moving around, finding objects."

"So," said Wepsiec, following up on Christenson's efforts to link falls, nonexistent skull fractures, and ear infections to retinal damage, "does swelling of the brain also cause the diffuse hemorrhages" found in Christopher's eyes?

"It rarely can," responded Lueder. Moreover, a retinoschisis cavity has never been described in a baby suffering just from swelling of the brain. Christenson's efforts to elicit admission that brain swelling or falling injuries could cause the acute retinal damage seen in Christopher were for naught.

The eye injuries sustained by Christopher were not an accumulation from repeated mild shaking; they were not caused by falls or now-you-see-them, now-you-don't skull fractures. And Lueder was firm about the time frame for Christopher's eye injuries: "It would have been some time between the person seeing him at 10:30 [that morning of August 3] and the time I saw him later that evening [at St. Louis Children's Hospital]."

Wepsiec put the same question to Dr. Kaufman.

> Q: Do you have an opinion based on a reasonable degree of medical certainty as to the time frame this injury was inflicted?
>
> A: It is acute in the order of hours . . . I mean, it happened to the best we could determine, within hours of our seeing the patient. . . . It would have to be after the child was last seen acting normally. . . . [I]t is just not medically possible for an injury such as that to persist for weeks to months and then suddenly cause this degree of brain injury.

Dr. Graham agreed with the other experts.

> Q: Do you have an opinion within a reasonable degree of medical certainty as to the time of the shaking or the acceleration/deceleration trauma?
>
> A: Yes. . . . Between eleven o'clock when the child was last seen to be normal and when the child arrived at the hospital.

The only person to have custody of Christopher from approximately 10:30 in the morning on August 3, 1994, to the time he was admitted to St. Joseph's was Gary Gould. A child who was described by Gary, Rhonda, and several other witnesses as "up around, walking, eating [on the morning of August 3], that's not a lethally injured, head-injured child," said Graham. In short, Christopher was fine until he was left alone with Gould; he had no old injuries that could account for the catastrophic damage he presented that morning. The only person who could have hurt him was Gary Gould.

While Kaufman and Lueder agreed they had no direct, eyewitness knowledge that Gould had shaken Christopher, Graham was unmovable in his testimony against Gould.

"Do you have any evidence to offer to the jury that my client shook this child?" Christenson asked.

"If he was in custody of the child when the child became symptomatic, then he shook the child," replied Graham, his tone intense and deliberate.

But perhaps it was Chuck Attig who stated the case most eloquently.

"[I]sn't it true that you had no concern that Gary would hurt your Christopher?" asked Christenson.

"I never suspected, no," was the heartrending reply.

"And is it also true that you have no direct information, even now, that he did hurt Christopher?" continued Christenson.

"Medical," replied Chuck, his tone dark and choppy.

"And what would that be, sir?" Christenson's voice was only nominally respectful. What, after all, could a big, stupid guy like Chuck Attig have understood about his son's injuries?

Chuck sat forward, his deep voice and broad shoulders leaning into his words, sending them with poignant intensity back to the lawyer: "Well, my son is dead. His eyes were shooken out of his head, disconnected."

Despite the parade of character witnesses for Gary, mostly former girlfriends, what could be said for him was that he had never been seen hurting a child and that he seemed to be fond of, or at least tolerated, the children with whom he had regular contact. Terry Hickam's father was brought in as a last-minute witness to say that Christopher was whiny that morning, which is exactly what everyone else said, including Gary and Rhonda.

Chuck Attig got recalled to explain how Rhonda picked Christopher up and let him down. She picked him up by "one arm and slid him up her right leg usually and then scooped underneath his butt." But the police interview showed Chuck using the word "shake," and Christenson kept trying to elicit this word from Chuck, who steadfastly corrected the unverified term. They did disagree over how she picked him up, but he didn't say "shake," he insisted, he meant "pull."

> Q: Did you make the statement to Detective Teas that Rhonda would shake and pull on Christopher when she should not have?
> A: I just explained that to you.
> Q: Did you make that statement, sir? It is not confusing. You're not confused, are you?
> A: Are you?

Chuck glowered at the lawyer, and several minutes later, with Christenson still after him on this point, he repeated, "We had a conflict on the way she picked him up."

"What didn't you like about it?"

"The first motion was just his arm, the weight [of] being picked up by his arm"—and here Chuck, never a wizard with words anyway, got exasperated—"then whatever, you know, you want to, I'll show you."

His tone was not friendly, and he twitched in the witness box as if he might get up and hoist the little lawyer up his leg and grab him by the seat of the pants. Christenson stepped back as Chuck maintained his seat and continued.

"She would scoop underneath his butt just like I told you earlier, and I didn't like it. But [Christopher] was at the age in April that he kind of liked it. . . . He liked the acrobatics."

But nothing—not Rhonda's bad temper and sporadic parenting, not falling, infections, or sleepiness, or even mysterious strangers in the night—could change the fact that the medical evidence against Gary Gould was overwhelming. I was curious about how Christenson was going to construct a closing argument, and I wondered if he could really think his client was innocent.

As I was to discover, the law prescribes a "zealous" defense, so Christenson proceeded through the closing arguments as if the medical experts had never testified. Dragging out the now legendary "long-term undiagnosed skull fracture" and the "accumulated fatal injury over time," he told us that Christopher was crying and whining that morning, refusing to engage in his normal play activities because — and here he corkscrewed dramatically down on one knee, miming the implied verbal action — "he was going comatose at this point and probably couldn't see as well." He assured us that we didn't have to think the doctors were lying to us in order to disregard their testimony in favor of the defense theories, but then attacked the coroner for ignoring the CT scan and urged us not to be "duped" by his testimony, as if he had, indeed, come here to deceive us.

Finally, to his credit, Christenson urged the jury not to "take it out on his client," if he, Christenson, had "acted in a manner you thought inappropriate." His words were timely, for several jurors did find the defense methods distasteful, citing the "dramatics" and Christenson's conduct as detracting from the argument being put before them.

Mike Wepsiec closed in his usual methodical fashion, the eloquence of the prosecution not in his stage presence or even his choice of words but in the careful, thoughtful organization of evidence. The facts spoke with an urgency that needed no costume or gesture. He reminded us of the crucial testimony from Gould that, in combination with the medical evidence, made him guilty of first degree murder:

> Q: [I]sn't it true that you know that shaking might cause injury to kids?
> A: Yes, sir, I do.
> Q: And you know that shaking might cause serious injury to those children?

A: Yes, sir.

Q: Isn't it true that you know shaking might cause the death of children:

A: Yes, sir—well, I would imagine it would if you shook them hard enough.

In order to convict Gould of first degree murder, the state had to prove that he took action he knew would cause death, or a strong probability of death or great bodily harm. As the charges were written by the state's attorney, intent was not at issue. As far as I could tell, then, Gould was guilty of first degree murder. But would my fellow jurors feel the same way?

The jury retired to deliberate the verdict at 10:55 A.M. on March 27, 1995. The three of us who were alternates were sequestered separately, admonished not to discuss the trial, and monitored by a bailiff. We had each brought some reading with us, but not eleven and a half hours' worth, which was how long it took for the jury to reach a verdict.

"I wonder what could be taking them so long," one of us would say loudly, as though the volume of our speech would trick the bailiff into thinking we weren't trying to communicate about the trial.

"I don't know," would be the response. "I sure know what I think about it."

We'd all nod knowingly.

"Yep, if it was us, we'd be done." We'd nod again. We all thought he was guilty, but we never had a chance to compare notes on which charge we'd prefer against him.

As the day wore on, we grew silent, worried about how long it was taking them to deliberate. Judge Watt circulated by periodically to regale us with stories of his exciting youth. We thumbed through old copies of *Field and Stream* and *Good Housekeeping* and took the *Cosmo* quiz on whether we still had sizzle in our relationships. We ate a bad, late lunch and a bad, late dinner. Like schoolyard truants, we took turns hanging out the second-story window, from which we could see the bank parking lot just opposite the courthouse. Our spirits sank when we saw Watt leave at dinnertime.

"Looks like we're in for it," I said.

"There's Chuck." We all clustered at the window. Chuck Attig strode across the parking lot and straddled his motorcycle, jumping up and down on it over and over, trying to start it. It teased, turning over, and then died. The March air was balmy and pure feeling, that early evening softness that comes only in the spring. A stream of fading gold light glinted across the coughing motorcycle and waffled along the shoulders of the lonely figure in the parking lot. He got off, looked around, shook his head, and, looking down at the ground, simply walked off.

"Looks like Chuck is having a bad day," someone said laconically.

"No fooling," was the reply. Then quietly we sat down again for more waiting.

We did not return to the courtroom until 10:40 P.M. We three alternates were seated first, looking like night creatures who had just been pried from under some rock and dressed in silly clothing. Then the jury filed in, and they looked even worse. Faces were pale and drawn, eyes ringed and dark, lipstick and any other routine primping long since forgotten. They turned one countenance toward the expectant courtroom: tense, anguished, exhausted. In the words of one juror, "It was hell. It was the most incredible thing I've ever had to do in my life."

In solemn, dramatic tones, Judge Watt read the verdict: "'We the jury find the defendant Gary Gould guilty'"—and he paused for just a moment—"'of involuntary manslaughter.'" Along with the collective sigh of exhaled breaths, a woman gasped audibly. Ruth Attig wept quietly.

Concerned about the question of intent, the jury had found itself unable to convict Gould of the more serious crime of first degree murder. At the same time, they did not want a mistrial, feeling such an outcome would be a great hardship for the families, so they compromised with the lesser conviction of involuntary manslaughter: Gary Gould was found guilty of acting in a reckless manner. He performed an act that caused great bodily harm and death by repeatedly shaking Christopher Michael Attig.

At the sentencing hearing, Ruth, Joyce, and Chuck read victim impact statements. Michael Wepsiec called for the maximum sentence allowed by law. Because Christopher was under the age of twelve years, and because Gould had committed a felony within the last ten years, Watt could sentence Gould for up to ten years in prison. Wepsiec noted that incarceration would not adversely affect Gary's ability to pay child support for his own daughter, because he hadn't paid child support since last June anyway—yet he'd been able to purchase a new Grand Prix in December. Flatly put, Gould's past criminal history, combined with the current homicide, did not suggest a promising future for him, and Wepsiec saw no mitigating reason why Gould shouldn't be sentenced to the full term allowed.

Paul Christenson argued for intensive probation. As he saw it, because Gary had one child die in his arms, it was unlikely he'd get himself into a similar situation. He advised the court that he would not trouble the proceedings with a stream of character witnesses to testify to what a good guy Gould was, although I found it hard to imagine just who those witnesses could possibly be. The bosses who fired him, or who saw him walk off the job? The ex-girlfriend still looking for child support payments? The persons he'd assaulted or threatened in his career as a local petty criminal? The undercover agent to whom he'd sold drugs?

Moreover, "I believe it is important not to let the histrionic testimony we have heard here this morning . . . unduly influence the court," Christenson proclaimed, referring to the victim impact statements. According to my dictionary, "histrionic" means "acting, the-atrical, dramatic behavior intended to impress people." That means that the only histrionics in the trial issued from Christenson, not the victims, and to characterize their testimony at any point in the pro-ceedings as "histrionic" revealed a disrespectful spirit animating the defense.

Then Gary had his turn: "I am not guilty, and I never harmed the child in any way, sir, and I don't really know what else to say. I have been put into this spot and I don't know how to deal with it. I never harmed the child in any way, sir. I never harmed any child in my life, and I am at the mercy of the court. And that's all I really have to say. Thanks."

No word of sorrow, no acknowledgment of Christopher, no sympa-thy extended to either family, no remorse but for himself, just the same words he'd mouthed from the beginning. Perhaps it was his negation of Christopher, his willingness to hide behind the body of the dead child — a child who could not have implicated him even if he had lived because he couldn't yet talk — that so angered me about Gould. Given the verdict of involuntary manslaughter, I wanted Judge Watt to apply the maximum penalty allowed by law.

He did.

"Christopher Attig is not here today because that boy couldn't de-fend himself," concluded Watt at the sentencing hearing. "But quite frankly, after listening to the testimony and evidence in the case, and reading the presentence report, I don't think the kid had a chance out-side of his grandparents. I really don't.

"Mr. Gould," continued Watt, "I am going to sentence you to ten years in the Illinois Department of Corrections."

Sitting almost directly in front of me was the Attig family. Chuck was holding a large framed picture of Christopher that was taken shortly before he died. Wearing his "My Grandpa Drives a Ford" t-shirt, Chris-topher is grinning big at the camera, showing all his baby teeth. As the verdict was read, Chuck looked down at the picture, tapped that round, happy face twice with his forefinger, then held the picture of his dead son close to his chest.

Joyce Lockhart was indignant about Judge Watt's pessimistic pronouncement about Christopher's chances. "Well, I think he was very wrong. Rhonda and Chuck have their bad points, but they both loved that baby dearly." To her, Christopher brought out the good in both Chuck and Rhonda. "And then, with Ruth's and my help, I do think Christopher stood a great chance, and I think Judge Watt misinterpreted the whole situation. There are a lot of children out there in much worse situations that nothing is being done about, and there are people raising their children who don't have the love that Christopher had just from his grandparents."

Rhonda and Chuck have vowed to keep an eternal flame burning in front of the little heart-shaped stone under the oak tree. Joyce visits periodically to clean the grave or leave some flowers, or just to sit and think. Ruth is there several times a week. "Maw Maw's here, Christopher," she calls out as she walks toward the secluded grave. She brings new decorations and books to read to Christopher. When Charlie is with her, he walks around, waiting, and then turns away as she leans over the stone to put her arms around its rough edges and press her warm lips again that cool, unyielding surface.

8

"The 'Nothing' Has Overcome This House"

We were cleaning windows on the front porch, and I suddenly stopped because there was a handprint on the window. It was so little. Then, I knew. It was so cool. It was Christopher's handprint, there on the window.

There are questions for which there likely will never be answers. Some of these questions involve nagging details: Why was a child who had been playing outside so utterly clean? Why was his clothing soaking in the bathtub? If he had been outside playing with the four-wheeler, why was it in the shed when the police arrived? Why was the trailer cleaned up? How long did Gary wait before calling for help?

We can imagine some logical answers. It's possible that Christopher was never taken outside that day and the four-wheeler was never removed from the shed in the first place. The only reason Gary had for placing Christopher outside in his version of events was so he could support the heatstroke story. Why had the trailer been cleaned up? Probably for the same reason Gary removed the marijuana plants from the back door. He'd allegedly been dealing drugs that morning, so cleansing the inside of the trailer of such material would be a logical move.

Why was Christopher so clean? Maybe because he'd had a bath with his mother that morning and he'd never been taken outside. Or, perhaps after Gary shook him, Christopher was bleeding or vomiting—common responses to shaking injuries—so Gary gave him another bath before calling for help. That might explain the clothing soaking in the bathtub.

There's no way of knowing when, between 10:30 A.M. and 12:30 P.M., to use the broadest possible time frame, Gary assaulted Christopher. But what usually happens in a fatal shaking is that the killer shakes the child violently and then throws him or her onto a couch or bed or against the floor or a wall. Sometimes that discard throw is part of the impact injury of Shaken Baby Syndrome. The child is stunned, may cry a little, and then becomes unconscious and then comatose within a few minutes. But an assailant would ignore the injured child and presume they were scared or sleeping. So, Gary may have thrown Christopher onto the couch and then left him there for as long as a hour, maybe more. Finally he notices that Christopher is too quiet—and that something is very wrong when he tries to wake him up. That would mean there was no dramatic collapse in the kitchen but only Gary's delayed, hysterical efforts at reviving a dying child.

Or, maybe in the first few minutes of the fatal injury, as his brain began to swell and lose function, Christopher tried to get off the couch and toddle toward Gary, only to collapse, face forward, in the kitchen. In the layout of the trailer it would have been only a few small steps from the couch to the kitchen. In Gary's version, he conveniently doesn't see the collapse. That would be too much like knowing the cause of the collapse, so in his staging, he has his back turned at the decisive moment. But that detail, the forward collapse, rings true. So maybe Gary didn't wait that long before calling for help. Unless, of course, he cleaned up the trailer before he called. Did Rhonda see blood on the kitchen floor, or did she see barbecue sauce? Or nothing at all?

The forward collapse rings as true as Rhonda's heart-wrenching image of Christopher waving bye-bye from the trailer door rings false, although I left it in the story because I wanted to believe in it. A nineteen-month-old can certainly wave bye-bye, but they usually do so in response to a prompt. The attention span necessary to keep a child that age at a door or window is a later development in a young child's repertoire of responsive social gestures. It's not impossible that Christopher was doing this, but it's not that likely, because Rhonda's usual method for leaving Christopher was for someone to distract him while she or the delivering caretaker sneaked out, because he cried. So Gould was probably telling the truth when he testified that the trailer door was closed because the air conditioning was on, and there was no made-for-TV bye-bye. But it also means it is unlikely that Gary, probably sleep-deprived and irritable and hung over, took the lonely little boy with an ear infection outside to play in the heat when he could lounge around in an air conditioned trailer. But maybe he was bored and did go outside with Christopher to hose off the patio.

It's also a reasonable guess that Gary lost his temper and that he intended to hurt and scare the child. Did he mean to kill Christopher? Given the way Wepsiec wrote the first degree murder charge, the question of intent is, legally speaking, irrelevant. Short of a miraculously candid confession, we have no way of knowing what he intended, any more than we have of knowing whether Gary was hung over or whether there was blood on the floor or whether Christopher really waved bye-bye. Given what has been omitted or fabricated, there is no way to account for everything. The story will always have gaps. All we can know beyond a reasonable doubt is that Gary Gould killed Christopher Michael Attig by shaking him to death.

And then there are the questions beyond these, the ones that no one can bear to contemplate. Did Christopher understand what was happening to him? Was he frightened? Did he cry? Was he in pain? Here is where the rational mind pulls up short, shies away, and refuses to take the next hurdle, and here is where most of us gratefully abandon the narrative trail. It is not our story.

But for Christopher's family, there is no stopping, no refusing that last terrible mental leap into the unknown of Christopher's fear and pain. Goaded by anguished hearts, their minds return ceaselessly to those unknown moments, repeatedly forced to travel a psychological territory beyond reasonable comprehension. Whatever the reality, living with this grieving imagination seems far worse. "I want to know so bad what really happened," says Rhonda. "It's just horrible not knowing what your child's last few hours were like, you know, and what must have run through his mind and how must he have felt, and was he scared."

"I've seen over and over in my head Christopher trusting him. Then [Gary] just picking him up and shaking him to a point where Christopher just goes unconscious and the last thing Christopher feels or knows is somebody that he trusted shaking him like that," says Chuck. "After the verdict came down, I tried to put Christopher to rest in peace," he continues, "but it wouldn't happen. Somebody would say something, or something would snap in my head, and I can see right now it's going to be years and years and years before Christopher is at rest, not out of my mind, but just at rest."

One of the saddest things I heard at Parents of Murdered Children was that the families of victims should never expect to find the truth from the trial, although this shouldn't be surprising. After all, the only person who could tell them everything is dead. All parents of murdered children find themselves tormented by mental images of their child's last moments and the terrible question of why. This is not something they choose to do; it is not a mental process that is amenable to rational discipline. It's simply now part of them, always.

Unfortunately, grieving is not an experience that usually brings people closer to one another, even within families who share a loss. As a culture, we allow people little space and time for grieving losses through death. People don't mean to be cruel, but significant grieving makes us uncomfortable. Perhaps there are too many pop psychology books on the market telling us there is an identifiable time frame for mourning. It is more convenient for us if the grieving person keeps it to himself or herself and gets over the loss efficiently, because we don't know how to respond.

The loss of a child under any circumstances, and at any age, is devastating, but people who have lost parents or siblings or friends and who have also lost children unanimously place that child loss in its own category. Recent grieving therapy is being restructured in recognition of the unique dimensions of child loss. As some experts describe it, the death of a child is "the worst loss, beyond endurance" (Rosoff, Knapp). The usual trajectories for healing simply don't apply, and well-meaning persons who advise suffering parents that "time will make a difference" or that "it's time to move on and get on with your life" only further wound the mourner with expectations they can't fulfill. Joyce was surprised at the silence of her coworkers after Christopher died, but "I think they didn't know what to say so they maybe felt better not saying anything or avoiding it." Ruth realized that she had done the same kind of thing to others, "because a lot of times I would pay my respects at the funeral in the morning when the family wasn't there. But since Christopher's death I have to personally tell them that I'm sorry for their loss, that I do know what it is."

Neither platitudes nor silence nor second-guessing the family constitutes appropriate responses to child death. Rather, they are self-serving responses that protect us and further isolate the grieving family. Some people told Ruth that "they would have killed Gary if Christopher had been their grandchild," which made Ruth feel like she was being judged again, that she wasn't a good grandmother and didn't love Christopher enough to murder Gary Gould. Joyce also felt pressure to take private action. With her prison connections, maybe she could put out a hit on him? But, as she said, "what kind of person would that make me? Wouldn't that make me the same kind he is, someone who doesn't value a life?"

Certainly Ruth struggled with her wish to kill Gary. One day shortly after Christopher died, Ruth was sitting in the truck in the Wal-Mart parking lot, waiting for Charlie. Looking up, she saw Gary. They crossed gazes, glaring. "I could have killed him and it would have been all over," she thought. Only later did she realize that she was sitting there with Charlie's loaded pistol right there in the truck cab.

Ruth told me she had figured out a way to take a gun into the courthouse, although she never did tell me if she had actually done so. But what she did say was that "I don't believe I would have ever thought of wanting to do anything so violent or vicious, but Christopher's death took out my heart where the love was and it's just filled with anger and bitterness and devious-type things I didn't think were capable of ever coming out of me."

The act of violence is like a perpetual robbery, with seemingly endless emotional repercussions, not a sentence of "ten years cut down to five, but for life," she says, referring to what will likely be Gary's actual time in jail. Even more horrible to her is the idea that "if Christopher could come in here right now, he wouldn't love the person I have turned out to be."

It is possible to survive the loss of a child, but you do not get over it. Like an amputee who still experiences the lost limb as a real, physical appendage, the family who has lost a child experiences the permanent presence of that child, the echoing space shaped of laughter and love. Like most amputees, parents learn to compensate, to love what is left and make the motions of caring where they are possible, to resume a reasonable life. But it can never be the whole life it once was because that beloved child will always be missing. Moreover, even parents of children who miraculously survive a shaking are plunged into this grieving process, for the healthy child they knew and loved has been taken from them, leaving them with a child who is forever changed by the abuse.

Any child death is untimely and fraught with anger and guilt, but the process of grieving is immensely complicated for families whose children die violently. For such families, there is no point at which we can locate a satisfactory point for closure — certainly not burial, and certainly not the trial itself. Indeed, the legal system is both avenger and tormentor for families of murdered children, and it becomes one of the further obstacles to healing. Almost immediately, the state steps in and takes their place as the injured party. The victims' families have no say about who represents them, and their feelings are excluded from the presumed objectivity of the legal process, their insights and experiences trimmed and shaped to fit the requirements of courtroom strategy.

While the family often struggles to get basic information about hearings and procedures, the killer is shielded by an intricate tangle of legal protections. The family may wait for the assigned trial date only to have the killer be granted a continuance, and so they must wait again, and sometimes again. Once in motion, the system that rightly proclaims the presumed innocence of the accused begins to seem constructed so exclusively for the convenience of the defense that one wonders that prosecution is even possible.

Although the presence of the victim's advocate in many prosecutor's offices has done much to assist parents of murdered children by accompanying the families of victims throughout the process and trying to make that process more friendly and intelligible to them, families are counseled by support groups such as Parents of Murdered Children not to expect relief from the judicial process by which the killer of their child is evaluated. If the jury delivers a strong verdict and the court a strong sentence, the family still must be on the alert throughout the appeals process, and then again for each parole hearing after that. Even those parents who follow the killer to the death chamber report that while they are relieved the killer of their child is dead, the execution cannot bring back their baby, and the pain is still always part of them.

The other prolonged complication for parents of murdered children is inherent in the swiftness and violence of the death. Unlike the circumstances surrounding other kinds of deaths, there has been no chance to prepare oneself and no chance to say good-bye. The death by violence is completely unnatural, gruesome in its details, both known and unknown, and families feel guilty about the things that, with the benefit of hindsight, they could have seen or could have said. The emotional rupture is so severe that surely it is understandable how the yearning heart returns endlessly to the scene of trauma, as if seeing it one more time in the eye of the heart would finally show something new, some clue, some small insight that would finally permit peace, or at least understanding.

From the point of view of the victims, justice is indeed a small, mean thing by the time they've been wrung dry by the system. In part, of course, they are asking the law to heal where it cannot, nor was it intended to do so. Even in the rare cases where a family agrees that justice is done, their hunger for completion and closure is not satisfied. The "why" of violent child death can never be satisfactorily answered by the legal system, which can only deliver human justice, not divine retribution. What, then, of religious and spiritual resources for the families of murdered children?

Here, too, the responses are equivocal. Some persons find consolation in their church community, although very few ever profess to understand why their child had to be taken from them. But life without God seems too terrible to contemplate, and so they are grateful for the presence of a religious community in their lives and find comfort in Scripture and prayer. Others, however, and this includes those who would have described themselves as strongly religious prior to the traumatic death, find no comfort in religious answers, and the loss of a satisfying spiritual life becomes one more consequence of the violence that robbed them of their child.

The members of the Attig and Carter/Lockhart families express a typical range of grieving and religious responses. Although no one claims to be a regular churchgoer, everyone in the Carter/Lockhart household believes in God and an afterlife. "I would say that when we go to church on Sunday, we're probably like millions of families across the world. We leave feeling a little closer, a little better about ourselves," says Joyce.

"Maybe I don't do it right, but I believe in God," reports Kevin. When Rhonda told Kevin that Gary was an atheist, "I knew he was worthless to begin with, and that just iced the cake. You know, weird shit happens when you don't believe in God, and that's just the way it is." Perhaps that belief is why Kevin hangs his head and mumbles boyishly when asked how he reconciled his belief in God with Christopher's death. "I kind of said some bad stuff about God," he confesses, and "I'll probably have to answer for it." Like everyone else, he wonders how such a senseless death could fit into a divine plan. "Everybody says, 'Well, God just wanted Christopher up there with him,' you know, and like, yeah, I have a hard time buying that one. But that's all there is, really," he trails off, his voice sad and quizzical, "that's all there is."

Joyce has been angry at God, but she is also confident that God is "a loving and forgiving guy. He's basically going to see me as a good person and help me through whatever I need to go through." She finds comfort in that belief, although she is quick to add that as for understanding the "why" of Christopher's death, "there's no answer and no comforting for that." Not surprisingly, she is brisk in her dismissal of precious religious explanations for this death. "Someone sent a poem after Christopher died about how God goes through and only picks very special children to be the littlest angels. Of course that was meant to comfort us, but I didn't find any comfort in that at all. This is a terrible thing to say, but there are other children out there [God could have chosen]." While she doesn't hold God responsible for Christopher's death, feeling that we are all given the ability to choose right or wrong, God seems remote to her, and she doesn't put much stock in trying to imagine an afterlife or Christopher in heaven. "I find that when I think about where Christopher's at or what he's doing, I find it really chilling, because I think he's in a cold grave instead of thinking about him being in heaven."

Chuck and Rhonda both think about Christopher as a spiritual presence in their lives. For Rhonda, he's "my personal little angel on my shoulder," and when they go to the cemetery to change the candles, Chuck talks to him, and "Christopher tries to keep Dad out of trouble." Similarly, Tim Attig feels that when he prays, God and Christopher are "watchin' out for me," and maybe Christopher is laughing, guarding his reckless uncle Tim from doing anything too stupid on his motorcycle.

Ruth, who is a Baptist (American), has tried to ease her grieving through prayer and reading of Scripture and inspirational literature. As a Christian, she felt assured that she would go to heaven and that her walk with God was clear and strong. But after Christopher died, "I never gave up on God, but it's like I thought he was punishing me for something," for why else would he have permitted such a horror, and then further compound the horror by refusing her prayer for a first degree murder conviction for Gary? She took some comfort in imagining that Christopher was a little angel in heaven and that when it was time to sleep, a big angel would sit by him and keep watch so he wouldn't be frightened in the darkness. She was also comforted by thinking that Christopher was such an energetic little angel that he had trouble keeping his halo on and had to chase it about, and when it rained "he's playing in God's water buckets."

But when she attended a talk about the afterlife at another church and confided her cherished mental images of Christopher to the minister, he dismantled her refuge for her. No, Christopher was not an angel, because "when people die they become spirits, and spirits are one step under Jesus, and angels are several steps under that." Further-

more, there is no big angel watching over Christopher at night, because there is no nighttime in heaven and nobody has any fears in
heaven anyway. Nobody sleeps there, and it's all "brilliant-bright all
the time."

But perhaps most distressing to Ruth was his pronouncement that
spirits age. Ruth hoped that when she died, she would be reunited with
her nineteen-month-old grandson. But according to this man, "spirits
continue to age, so if I don't die for twenty years, then Christopher will
be twenty-one" when they are reunited, and she will have missed
twenty years of his being.

God has always answered her prayers, and she freely acknowledges
that until now, God has blessed her life. But when she expressed her
puzzlement over his silence now, after praying for comfort and for a
first degree murder conviction for Gary, Ruth received two troubling
responses from friends. One was the pat formula, "He has answered
your prayer, and the answer is no." Sensible Ruth immediately wonders why after all these years of being with her, God chose now to say
no. And even if no is the answer, what meaning is she supposed to de-
rive from it? "No, I am punishing you for unspecified sins"? "No, I
don't care about small children"? "No, I'm tired of answering your
prayers"? "No, I have another plan in mind, but I'm not telling you
what it is"?

The other response is that she will be without God as long as she
cannot forgive Gary and Rhonda for Christopher's death. The hospital
chaplain assures her that her forgiveness for Gary and Rhonda is not a
precondition for God's healing presence, but most of her religious
counselors advise her that God will be absent to her as long as she feels
vengeful. Perhaps more than any other religious question, this is an in-
surmountable obstacle to her. "I know we're not supposed to question
God, but when a beautiful baby is killed and there are so many vile,
evil people left on earth, I question it. For me to forgive is like saying
it's okay that Gary killed Christopher, and I just don't see how God ex-

pects me to say it's okay to take an innocent baby's life." Although well-meaning pietists assure her that if she asks for forgiveness, God will be right there, literalist that she is, Ruth takes the motions of grace seriously. "I could ask, but my heart knows I don't mean it, so why lie to God? He would know I didn't mean it."

What to do when religious responses can't soothe the cry of the suffering heart? Ruth has no answer for this. Each day, she renews her spiritual struggle, painstakingly sifting through the pain and horror of the last year, desperate to discover some of the peace the Bible seems to promise for the brokenhearted. Each day, her relationship to God shifts, and shifts again. She wants so much to believe in something better than what grips her now.

The night before the sentencing, Ruth went to Christopher's grave and "hollered out at God just like what they did in the Bible. I was going down to kill myself, and I cried out to him and he didn't answer my prayer. I know that just because you holler out to God [it] doesn't mean he has to answer your prayer, but I am consumed with the fact that Christopher didn't mean anything to God." And yet, perhaps she can hope otherwise, because after all, "I know he loved him because he called him home rather than have him remain here [with such terrible injuries]." So, for now, the best she can do is try to get through each day and say to those who tell her it's time to put aside her anger and forgive "that when they put my shoes on and when they invade this body and know the hurt of this heart and what I have gone through, then they can tell me what to do, but not until."

"We barely make it through the day," Joyce testified at the sentencing hearing. "My son is failing in school, and I can't hold down a job. Kevin is bitter and cranky, and we don't sleep well. Rhonda and Robyn are drinking too much and missing work and school." In fact, for a time, the household scattered, with Kevin moving out for a week, Buddy going to live with relatives, and Rhonda moving in with her aunt. Kevin told Joyce it was even difficult to walk into the house. "It was like the 'nothing' has overcome this house," she says, borrowing a phrase from the movie *The NeverEnding Story*.

Everyone has a different way of coping with grief. But how does one understand and reconstruct a life after a death such as this one?

Rhonda

There's never a day that goes by since all of this has happened that I don't have it on my mind, Gary and Christopher and everything that's happened. I knew when I started going out with Gary that he was a wild one, but I didn't think he was, like, cruel or mean or anything. I mean, if you could have seen Gary before Christopher died and just how he was with his dog, I mean, just everything. It's beyond me how he could go into court and sit there so self-centered, more worried about his looks than anything. It pissed me off, is what it did, him flipping me off and stuff, and sometimes he would look at me like "I'm sorry," but for the most part he had this attitude of Mr. Billy Badass. And I thought, you know, you're here on trial for the murder of a baby, you idiot, and you don't come in here acting as if it's no big deal, because you're making an ass of yourself, is what you're doing. He really disgusted me, and I was really ashamed to have been his girlfriend.

I believe that everything happens for a reason and there is going to be a day when I'm going to find out why this happened, and then I'll understand. I don't think God did it to be mean. Maybe he did it to make an example for other people, and maybe it will save other children's lives. We're supposed to learn something and try to do better. I have been given a second chance, and I'm taking it pretty serious, you know, to try to do the best I can. God's only going to give me one life. I can do it the right way or I can do it the whole wrong way, and I know what the wrong way is. I've paid for the wrong way. I don't have my son, and that is like, oh, that is the worst thing in the world. Partying all the time doesn't get you anywhere, and you think at the time, "I can fix it later." Well, you know, you've got to fix it today or it's never going to get any better.

Yeah, I'm totally different than I was before. I don't drink really anymore — if I do drink I drink maybe two drinks [and] I'm done; I just don't do drugs anymore; I go to church; I'm paying my bills; I've kept my job. I'm going back to school, you know. I was a nursing major, and I'm only twenty-three so I'm still going to go back, because I like to work with children. I can't have any more children. My mom is a nurse and she used to love to work with children, and she can't handle it at this point in her life, but I'm sure within the next four or five years she'll be back working with children because that's what she loves, and I think by the time I finish school I'll be ready. Gary always told me — and Chuck did too — that I was a big baby because I was always talking to my mom, but I'm just like that with my mother. And I'll probably live here for a while, you know.

I know I've done bad things and I know some things aren't the way I should have done things. My biggest mistake was that I didn't spend enough time with just me and Christopher, and I know that there isn't one of us who'll ever know another day like those we shared with Christopher. I hope there will never be a day that passes that Gary will cease to remember Christopher before his death . . . and then live with his mental image of him lying there dying because of what he's done. I've been judged a lot in the last year, and I know I did a lot of things wrong, but I only wish that everyone could crawl inside my heart so they'd know how I've been feeling. I'll be forever missing my little boy.

Joyce

I think Gary cannot face the fact of what he's done. Christopher learned to say "Gary" before he learned to say "Daddy," and I know in my mind that Gary loved him. If I could say anything to Gary, I would look him in the eye and tell him, "You have betrayed us, and for that betrayal I cannot ever forgive you."

We allowed him to come to this home and stay, and in front of Murphysboro society's eyes, we stood behind him. Had he ever looked at Rhonda in the beginning of this, had he said, "Oh, my God, look what I've done, I'm sorry," everyone in this house would have fought with the entire area and helped them work through their relationship. We would have seen to it if that was what Rhonda wanted. There is not one person in this house that believes that Gary Gould got up that day and decided to kill Christopher, but we do believe Gary killed Christopher, that he lost control, and he did it.

It's going on almost a year later and we're somewhat moving forward, but we're not seeing any children in our future, and that is pretty devastating to me. Christopher was the thing that brought this entire family together. Now I grieve for my twenty-three-year-old daughter, who can have no more children. Every now and then I get this thought that we can go out of the country and adopt. I have friends who adopted in Peru and China, and you know those children are from such underprivileged countries; I think we could do wonderful with a child like that. But then I think I'm talking about adopting with Rhonda, and that is not realistic. I don't want anything to take away from my grief, not that I enjoy my grief, but my grief for Christopher is very much a part of me, and I am still grieving, and I'm not ready to stop for a baby to come along. I've always done pediatric and dialysis-type work, and home health was pediatric cases, and now I will not work with children. I did take one case with a little girl on a vent, and she looked like Christopher. She spent a lot of time in [St. Louis] Children's Hospital, and the nurses wrote wonderful notes in her little book. Except I thought of Christopher, who was there under such terrible circumstances, and I remember the nurses looking at us like, "Which one of you did this?" And there was no little notebook for Christopher, because they didn't know him. I bawled the entire night, went home, and called up and said I will not work on another case with an infant. I'm going to work with the elderly.

One day after Christopher died, Rhonda told me about a dream that kept coming back. In the dream I'm real old, like ninety-seven, and she's eighty. I was seventeen when I had her, you know. And in the dream we're standing over Robyn's grave, next to Christopher's, and Kevin's grave, and Buddy's grave. It's just me and her.

I don't know that Rhonda will ever really move away from me, probably not.

Robyn

It was devastating, absolutely devastating. I got to the point where I was like, I just don't care. I took a semester off from school, and I got very behind on my bills, and in my job that I was doing well in, I didn't care anymore. When I did go back to school, I did awful. Now it's a year later and I'm just now getting to a point were I can say, "All right, Robyn, you're not like this, you've got to get out of this rut you're in."

Everybody wanted to see Gary get convicted of first degree murder, but I think it was just because everyone was angry. I think when he did it, he didn't realize. But Gary was not man enough to say, "I'm so sorry your baby is dead. This was an accident and I'm willing to take whatever punishment I have to." I really think that's all my sister wanted him to do.

I loved Gary, and just to see him sitting in that courtroom in the situation made me want to cry. There were a few times when Gary and I made eye contact in there, and I wanted to go up to him and say, "Gary, I'm so sorry you are in this position now. I don't know what to do for you, but I just want you to know that my heart goes out to you because I am sorry." But I never could have done that because Gary couldn't do me the same courtesy of saying, "Robyn, I'm sorry you lost your nephew who I know you were very close to." Because I felt like Christopher's other mother, you know. I watched that little boy grow in every way and I'll never forget anything and I'll never regret anything I ever did for him because I loved that little boy with all my heart.

Tim

I still want children sometime down the road. I really did bad after Christopher was gone. In fact I talked to my mom and said I just wanted to pay someone to have my baby and then leave me alone so I would never have any problems [and keep my baby safe].

Debbie

Some things that were important to me don't seem so important now. I used to think it was important that I had my nights out to myself with girlfriends or whatever, and I don't care for bar scenes anymore. Both my children loved Christopher. The minute I told my seven-year-old what had happened, she cried and she was immediately sorry for the mean things she'd done, like taking a toy away from him. My teenage son is still very angry, and for a long time I found myself reassuring my daughter that I love her. She still remembers Christopher and talks about him.

I did a lot of my grieving by myself for Christopher because I felt like it was important for me to be there for Chuck and hold my feelings in and just let them out elsewhere when I could. I wish Gary had been man enough to say what happened and be sorry for it. I just hope he thinks about it every day, you know? I hope it dwells in his mind forever.

Ruth

The only way that I can cope with life and keep going is I have to tell myself daily [that] as much as I loved Christopher, he's better off dead because he didn't stand much of a chance to lead what I would consider a decent life. But I wish God would have chose something different than having him be murdered, because I still don't know—did Christopher feel it, did he cry, did he lay there in pain? I guess the only thing I could have done to save him from the life he was leading and his upcoming death would have been to have stole him and stayed on the move until I ran out of money.

With the life-styles that some young parents choose now, with the partying and drugs so prevalent, I would beg the young girl to give her child to someone else to take care of, whether it be her mother, her aunt, even the boy's parents, with some kind of legal understanding that when you get your head on straight and you realize that drugs and wild parties isn't the way to go, then you can have your baby back. Here are these innocent little beings that look to the adults for not only their meals, but their protection, their care, their love, just everything. That's how God meant it to be. You can teach them what you hope is right and teach them morals in a loving way, or you can completely ignore them and cuss them and knock them around, and that's what they will learn in turn to do, and that's the kind of parent they'll be. Just because they're little, they don't vote yet, they don't hold a job, but children are our future and we can't go on murdering our future.

We all wonder what we're put here on earth for, and I just always felt mine was to take care of babies. No child could ever be as dear to me as Christopher was. I'm not saying that in later years I won't be capable of loving another child. But Christopher, I felt like he was mine because I had him so much. Being a grandmother to a little angel like my Christopher was just the best icing in the world on the most beautiful cake.

I guess everyone wants to feel needed, and I don't feel like my boys need me anymore. But Christopher needed me, and it was a love I put a 150 percent into. And maybe that's why it hurts so bad. I know we're only supposed to take one day at a time, but it's hard not to think, like we did last summer, to think what we would do this summer. I should have been happy with what we were doing last summer, instead of looking forward to all the things we could do when Christopher was a little older. If we didn't look ahead, maybe we wouldn't realize so much what we had lost.

We never did get to film Christopher with the squirrels, but Mom said that she gives them extra peanuts and tells them, "These are from Christopher."

Chuck

Since my boy died I couldn't tell you the half. My life has been a blur, and I have done a lot of ignorant things, out running with my head left at home, and I didn't care. Gary took the only thing from me that was me, because I don't know my background on my bloodline. I knew Christopher was mine because me and Rhonda didn't have no outs to where it was a possibility that it could have been somebody else's. He was just too much like me.

If I had it to do all over again, I want to begin with a bank account before I was settled down with somebody and have everything to where there wasn't any friction. Wouldn't that be cool? You know, you go ahead and deal with it your way and I'll deal with it mine and just leave me alone, no strings attached, but still working towards a nice home and money in the bank. And then that way whenever you decide to have a kid it's like all corners are hemmed up, you know? Because having Christopher with the woman I had him with was just about the craziest thing I've ever went through. It's not like you see on TV shows where it just goes as smooth as a blade.

I put him on my skin, "Christopher Michael Attig R.I.P.," and then he always loved my bulldogs. It's something I can look at everyday, and it means something to me. The saying on this one here [bulldog tattoo on his upper arm] is for me; it says, "The strong will survive."

I wish I could give up something in my life just to have him back if it was just . . . I've even thought if it was just to see him grow up to three or four. You know? Just give up something of mine. But it don't go that way.

9

Shaking Is No Accident

*I remember him in his little swimming trunks outside play-
ing, and the way he would smile and the way that he gritted
his teeth. Eating banana . . . it would get all over his face
and he'd smush it in his hands.*

Within a half an hour of entering deliberations, nine of the
jurors were confident that Gary Gould was guilty of killing
Christopher Attig. Of the three with doubts, one had reservations about the medical evidence, one seemed to have more in
common with Gary Gould than the dead child, and one, according to
a fellow juror, was "overeducated beyond his intelligence and seemed
to think he was in an episode of *Murder, She Wrote*." This last juror finally changed his mind, leaving the other two to wrestle with whether
or not they were experiencing reasonable doubt.

"We were all very supportive of each other, and it was good to see
how strangers could be put in a room together like that and be so personal and caring. Everybody was really careful not to criticize and
[tried to] understand why the person thought this way," reports juror
Melody Chamberlin. Even jurors who were firmly convinced Gould
was guilty wavered in their conviction about which charge to sustain
against him, so, given the juror dynamics, a compromise verdict of involuntary manslaughter seemed reasonable to them, especially after
eleven and a half hours of deliberation. No one wanted a mistrial.

After the jury reported its verdict, Judge Watt asked them to recon-vene in the jury room, along with the alternates. It's something he al-ways does with a jury, to give them a chance to ask questions and pro-cess the event of the trial. Almost in one voice, they asked him, "Did we reach the right verdict?"

"Whenever a jury reaches a verdict, it's the right verdict," he replied. More than one juror expressed gratitude for his reassurance. Haunted by what they had heard and emotionally exhausted by the trial and their own arduous process of decision making, they needed confirma-tion that they had honorably fulfilled their service.

Later, I asked Watt if he felt that involuntary manslaughter was the most appropriate verdict in the case.

"No," was the answer, much to my surprise. He clarified. "Given the facts of the case, based on the jury instructions, yes, the verdict was appropriate. No, in the sense that I think Mr. Gould needed a longer sentence, but I didn't have an option. I wish there had been something in between, because I think this was a little more than involuntary. There needed to be something between involuntary manslaughter and murder. But there was no niche." He went on to comment that had the jury found Gould guilty of first degree murder, he believed the ap-pellate court would have upheld that verdict. As it was, the Fifth Dis-trict Appellate Court upheld Gary Gould's involuntary manslaughter conviction. In an order filed on November 22, 1996, the court com-mented that "the evidence presented against defendant at trial was overwhelming."

Because Gould had a prior felony conviction, Watt was able to sen-tence him to the maximum penalty under Illinois law for involuntary manslaughter, ten years. But because of day-for-day credit for good be-havior, it appears that Gould will serve less than five years of that sen-tence. Five years for killing a child? Gould clearly said he knew that shaking a baby could cause harm or death. If the jury thought he was guilty of killing Christopher, then by his own admission he had acted more than recklessly: he had acted knowingly. Why did they find it so difficult to convict him of first degree murder?

Well, for one thing, although juror Norm Flannagan was skeptical about the defense portrait of Gould as a loving stepfather and family baby-sitter, there was no dramatic history of neglect, abuse, or assault admitted into evidence, making it more difficult to comprehend his role in the death. And yet, according to St. Louis County Coroner Dr. Michael Graham, children most commonly die "from injuries received during a single assaultive episode" (Monteleone and Brodeur, 431). Gould's fatal assault of Christopher may have been that single episode. In suspected cases of SBS, however, it is crucial for families and investigators to be alert to subtle evidence of earlier shaking, because 71 percent of SBS victims have suffered prior abuse, and "it is clear that children are usually shaken on several other prior occasions before one episode is so severe as to require medical attention" (Alexander and Smith, 3).

Secondarily, the jury also agonized over the imagined consequences for Gould should they convict him of first degree murder. "We had a man's life in our hands. We thought we were hanging him. Gas chamber or something," was one comment. That is, although jury instructions told them they were not to worry about the sentencing, they did. It's an understandable concern, but it also demonstrates how the living can preempt the claim of the victim in the judicial process.

But there were other factors involved that mimic a nationwide pattern of decision making in child death cases. *A Nation's Shame* clearly spells out the impediments to successful prosecution of child death. The three biggest problems are (1) prosecutors and judges who are not sufficiently educated about child abuse deaths and who fail to pursue full recourse of the law, (2) juries who are not sufficiently educated about child abuse deaths and who refuse to believe the evidence before them, and (3) laws that are inadequate for the manner in which child abuse deaths are perpetrated. In the Attig case, the state's attorney used the law available to prosecute Gould for the maximum penalty, first degree murder. But the jury was not ready to follow his lead because they just didn't believe Gould had meant to harm Christopher. Leslie Warner expresses what I heard several times from jurors: "I guess he was a substitute father for the child a lot of the time. Most parents wouldn't take their own . . . child and kill them on purpose. So that's how we determined he did it, but he didn't mean to do it."

This comment presents more than one questionable assumption. The first is that most parents wouldn't kill their own children. Unfortunately, parents are the persons most likely to kill children. Let me repeat the gruesome statistic cited in the introduction to this book: 80 percent of abused children are harmed by parents; 10 percent are harmed by caretakers related to them. Every year, two thousand children die of abuse and neglect; 90 percent of them were killed by a parent or relative.

The second problematic assumption concerns intent. One does not need to prove intent in order to convict someone of first degree murder in Illinois, and the charges were written so as to exclude intent as a debatable item. Gould was charged with knowingly taking action that could cause great harm or death. Nonetheless, the Attig jury found themselves unable to avoid speculation about what Gould intended to do that morning, and they found it implausible that Gould intended to kill Christopher. I agree with them. I don't think Gary Gould got up on the morning of August 3, 1994, saying to himself, "Today I'm going to kill Christopher." But an intentional action is different from a knowing action. Citing two recent studies, *A Nation's Shame* advises us that "many fatal injuries must result from very violent attacks, suggesting that many parents are conscious of the damage they are inflicting" (15). The American Academy of Pediatrics statement on shaking in *Pediatrics* has become a guiding definition in Shaken Baby Syndrome literature: "While caretakers may be unaware of the specific injuries they may cause by shaking, the act of shaking/slamming is so violent that competent individuals observing the shaking would recognize it as dangerous" (872). That is, the adult may not intentionally set out to kill

a child, but he or she initiates action they recognize as dangerous—
action that might produce great bodily harm or death.

Unfortunately, this understanding has yet to inform the legal system. When six-foot, three-hundred-pound David McGuigan killed his
seven-week-old son by shaking in 1990, Chicago prosecutors argued he
was guilty of first degree murder. But a Cook County judge ruled that
his actions were unintentional and convicted him of involuntary manslaughter. And in May of 1994, the Illinois Appellate Court overturned
the first degree murder conviction of Stephen Holmes, arguing that he
did not know he could kill or seriously injure his six-month-old baby
when he shook her.[1] How could any adult who understands the fra-
gility of a baby, who routinely supports that baby's head when carrying
or playing with him or her, then violently shake that same ten- to
fifteen-pound child and claim they didn't know that what they were doing could be dangerous? Are we really to believe that when six-foot,
185-pound Gary Gould picked up 35-pound Christopher Attig—who
was a hefty toddler—and shook him so violently he suffered irrevers-
ible brain damage, the shaking was "involuntary"? Accidental? It took
sustained, deliberate strength to injure Christopher fatally.

Whether or not the parent picked up the child with the explicit intention of killing is simply not germane to these cases, as it was not germane in the Attig case. At the least, the enraged adult means to hurt
and scare that child. "Some experts postulat[e] that shaking is primarily a result of anger felt by an adult, combined with loss of impulse control, and that the perpetrator is aware of its potential to harm children.
Other experts suggest that, while frustration is an element of shaking,
lack of knowledge about its dangers may be a contributing factor."[2] But

1. Janan Hanna, "'Shaken Baby' Death Ruled Manslaughter," *Chicago Tribune*,
February 2, 1994, 1.

2. Jacy Showers, *The National Conference on Shaken Baby Syndrome: A Medical,
Legal, and Prevention Challenge*, Executive Summary (Alexandria, VA: National Association of Children's Hospitals and Related Institutions, n.d.), 213.

while an adult may not understand the specific mechanism of fatal injury, any reasonably intelligent adult is responsible for recognizing that what he or she is doing is dangerous. Shaking is a deliberate assault. The Attig jury is not alone in its refusal of the deliberate nature of shaking assault. In a 1993 case of SBS in San Diego, Randell Alexander, a University of Iowa expert on the syndrome, explained what had happened to thirty-eight-day-old Christopher Monroe at the hands of his father, Robb Haggett, accused of second degree murder. Alexander demonstrated the force necessary to produce fatal shaking injuries using a Little Baby Water Babies doll. "He held the doll only inches from his face, squeezed its chest, then began shaking the doll in a grotesque way. The shaking lasted less than 10 seconds until the doll's head popped off and rolled across the courtroom. 'If you're going to kill a child, you're going to have to give it everything you've got,' Alexander said as he walked back to the witness stand."[3] A month later, jurors found Haggett innocent.

In another case of SBS in North Carolina, Alexander testified about the fatal injuries sustained by a sixty-two-day-old infant whose caretaker reported that the child's injuries, including rib and skull fractures, were caused by falling off a couch. The child died of brain damage. The jury found the man not guilty. "People are inclined to not want to believe in child abuse anyway," Alexander said. "They would like to believe that little things can cause these kinds of damage."[4]

A Nation's Shame cites the case of an Oklahoma mother who asked her boyfriend to babysit for her infant girl. "While she was gone, the boyfriend became enraged over the baby's crying and violently shook the child until the infant was dead. An autopsy revealed severe brain damage caused by shaking. After the boyfriend's arrest, a photograph of

3. "Debate Grows over Causes of Shaken Baby Syndrome," *Houston Chronicle*, June 27, 1993, sec. A, 5.

4. Karen Brandon, "State to Erase Play as Shaken Baby Cause," *Chicago Tribune*, August 26, 1993, 1.

him ran in local newspapers showing him wearing a cap popular in Oklahoma that read, *Number One Dad*. At his trial, the man admitted he had attacked the child, but the jury found him not guilty. Later, the district attorney was criticized for charging the boyfriend with first-degree murder, since the jury was not able to accept the killing as premeditated" (57).

It is not only juries who refuse to see, however. In the recent, highly publicized Massachusetts case of au pair Louise Woodward, the jury reached a unanimous verdict of second degree murder for her role in the shaking and slamming death of eight-month-old Matthew Eappen, only to see it replaced by the judge's view of things. Taking primary inspiration from his compassion for the defendant, Judge Hiller B. Zobel reduced the murder conviction to involuntary manslaughter and then sentenced the unrepentant young woman to time served.

According to the Executive Summary of the *National Conference on Shaken Baby Syndrome*, "a major obstacle in adjudicating these cases is denial among the public that anyone would shake a baby violently enough to cause severe injury or death, as well as denial within individual families that loved ones would do this."[5] Jury disbelief is one of the key elements in protecting child killers. Why is child killing unbelievable to juries? I've had several reasons suggested to me, some of them cynical comments on human nature. In the case of shaking, juries may hesitate to convict someone for an activity that jury members themselves may have indulged in. They shook their kids; to convict someone else for shaking is to admit, at least privately, to their own harmful behavior. Or, perhaps despite nationwide language about "family values," we don't really think that children's lives are that important. For some adults, children are more an abstraction, a nuisance, a small form of human property with little tangible reality to them.

Undoubtedly, these things are sometimes factors. But I still find my

5. Showers, *National Conference*, 20.

original argument most compelling. We don't want to see what adults deliberately do to children. It's just too awful. We'd rather think it was an accident, at worst, adult recklessness. This seems to be especially true for shaking deaths because we are asked to comprehend that a caretaker can deliberately kill a child using nothing more than his or her bare hands.

If this is difficult for juries and judges, it has been equally problematic for medical professionals. A recent, dramatic example of how child killers are protected by our refusal to see is documented by Richard Firstman and Jamie Talan in *The Death of Innocents*. In this riveting and comprehensive study of Sudden Infant Death Syndrome, Firstman and Talan show how SIDS became a cover for homicide by smothering. Medical researchers and attending physicians failed to take cognizance of or simply refused the evidence before them, and what were once hailed as landmark studies of SIDS now appear to be the unwitting chronicle of how, in some cases, disturbed parents perpetrated multiple murders of young children.

Firstman and Talan do not discuss shaking in their book, but SBS researchers have already suggested that a death certificate designation of SIDS may be covering up shaken baby homicides as well.[6] Like smothering, shaking a child to death can leave few external injuries. Without an autopsy, the crime may be undetected.

Indeed, the typical SBS defense — and the Gould defense was an excellent example — takes full advantage of the unique nature of shaking assaults by playing upon jury willingness to avoid confrontation of adult cruelty. Even the term "shaking" belies the violence of the action and the severity of the injuries produced. One of the most common strategies is to suggest to juries that the shaking injuries are the product

6. See M. Bass, R. E. Kravath, and L. Glass, "Death-Scene Investigation in Sudden Infant Death," *New England Journal of Medicine* 315 (July 1986): 100–105; Jacy Showers, "'Don't Shake the Baby': The Effectiveness of a Prevention Program," *Child Abuse and Neglect* 16 (1992): 11–18.

of earlier, trivial falls. Kirschner and Wilson list the most common implausible stories offered by parents and caretakers to explain lethal injuries, including falls from low heights, such as from a couch or down
a flight of stairs; a fall where the child's head strikes a hard object, like
a coffee table; injury inflicted by an older sibling; and injury caused by
aggressive resuscitation when the child "suddenly stopped breathing."
There are no documented cases of children dying from SBS by falling
two feet from a couch, four feet from Daddy's arms, or even ten feet
down the stairs, and yet these kind of explanations are so predictable
that Kirschner and Wilson have labeled the deadly items of furniture
"killer couches," commenting that "it is discouraging to see how often
these stories are still accepted at face value by physicians, other health
care professionals, and child protection workers" (329-30).

Without a confession, nearly all SBS cases are circumstantial and
depend primarily upon medical evidence to locate the assailant. Thus,
another common defense strategy is to question the medical time
frame by suggesting that the child was shaken by someone other than
the defendant, many hours or days prior to the actual collapse of the
child. Here is where SBS defenses find an effective wedge and where
more research and public education are needed.[7] SBS experts appeal
to both medical evidence and common sense in establishing a time
frame. A child who is hit by a car at 10:00 A.M. does not suddenly show
symptoms of severe crash injury late in the afternoon; the symptoms
present immediately. A child who is severely or fatally shaken on a
Tuesday does not remain functional until Wednesday and then suddenly collapse. When the shaking is violent, producing severe trauma,
the symptoms present at once. In very young children and babies,
"lethal injuries produce progressively more severe symptoms almost

---

7. Marcus B. Nashelsky and Jay D. Dix, "The Time Interval Between Lethal Infant
Shaking and the Onset of Symptoms," *American Journal of Forensic Medicine and Pathology* 16, no. 2 (1995): 154–57.

immediately; no significant 'lucid' or asymptomatic period occurs," and "in general, the more severe the trauma, the more precisely it can be dated."[8]

A third typical defense is perhaps the boldest of all. The implicated caretaker professes astonishment over the child's injuries. The child was normal at one hour and found comatose at another hour. How the child could be suffering from subdural hematoma, cerebral edema, and retinal hemorrhages — the diagnostic triad for SBS injuries — with no discernible cause is just one of those mysteries of life. The denial of the caretaker then circles back to one of the earlier defense strategies: Perhaps these fatal injuries were caused by a fall suffered earlier in the week? Perhaps someone else shook the child at an earlier time and the injuries are just now appearing?

Like most child death cases, SBS cases are difficult to prosecute. There are seldom witnesses or confessions; so much depends upon the medical evidence and the willingness of juries to see what goes on. "Prosecutors all over the country will tell you that the easiest murder to get away with is the killing of an infant or small child by a parent or caretaker."[9] That's why seeing what happened to Christopher is so important. Until we start seeing and hearing, we can't change the future for other young children like him.

One recent effort at seeing and hearing occurred November 10–12, 1996, in Salt Lake City. There, the first National Conference on Shaken Baby Syndrome brought parents of SBS children together with medical, legal, and social services experts for an intensive conference dedicated to disseminating information about SBS and working toward better coordinating the network of professionals needed to prevent or prosecute SBS assaults. Several important recommendations emerged from this conference, which I combine here with my reading

8. Kirschner and Wilson, 350; Levitt, Smith, and Alexander, 18.
9. *A Nation's Shame*, 58.

of the growing literature on SBS and other forms of child abuse assaults.

1. *Shaking must be legally recognized as a form of deliberate assault uniquely practiced upon young children.* This can be accomplished by writing law that takes into account child abuse as a form of homicide. In *A Nation's Shame,* the U.S. Advisory Board on Child Abuse and Neglect recommends that "[s]tates should enact 'felony murder or homicide by child abuse' statutes for child abuse and neglect. States that currently define child abuse as a misdemeanor should establish laws to define child abuse and neglect as felonies" (xxxix). In Illinois child endangerment is a misdemeanor with a maximum penalty of 364 days in jail and up to a $1,000 fine, regardless of whether a child is unharmed, injured, or killed. Pending legislation initiated by State's Attorney Michael Wepsiec, and cosponsored by state Senator David Luechtefeld and Representative Michael Bost would make fatal child endangerment a Class 3 felony, punishable by two to five years in prison.

Furthermore, the law needs to recognize that young children are not killed by the usual methods of deliberate mayhem used against older children and adults, such as shooting and stabbing. Young children often die in ways that could be construed as accidental or "involuntary" by their assailants and by other adults unwilling to acknowledge the pernicious dimensions of violent child death. SBS must be identified as a child abuse injury, as two states already do. In Kansas, shaking constitutes child abuse felony, and in Utah, the definition of "serious physical injury" includes the brain swelling caused by shaking. This kind of legal definition may be especially important for those instances when premeditation, or intent, becomes a stumbling block to prosecution. Although there will always be gray areas that the law cannot reasonably anticipate in every specific case of child injury, we can do a better job of holding adults of normal intelligence accountable for their actions (or in the case of death by neglect, inaction). Let the law recognize that shaking a child is an assault so violent that "competent individuals observing the shaking would recognize it as dangerous."

2. *We must develop a thorough and systematic nationwide "Don't Shake the Baby" campaign.* No one who smokes can claim they don't know that smoking is a dangerous activity. Likewise, no one who cares for children should be able to claim that they didn't realize the harm of shaking. If common sense cannot be relied upon, let a national saturation of information about SBS make this excuse unbelievable.

Recent studies enable us to identify at-risk audiences. A *Nation's Shame* points out that although mothers are often accused in abuse and neglect deaths, in fact, the "adult most dangerous to an infant or small child is male" (13), with female baby-sitters close behind (Starling et al.). Prevention programs, such as "Healthy Families America," suggest creative approaches for reaching potential abusers. "Healthy Families Arizona" screens families at risk for child neglect and domestic violence and offers up to five years of regular home visits. These visits provide emotional support, child development information, and opportunities for parents to learn bonding behaviors with their children. Of the high-risk families screened for this program, 95 percent accepted services. In these families, there was no abuse or neglect reported for 97 percent of the infants involved, and health care was provided for 100 percent of the infants involved.

In Utah, the Child Abuse Prevention Center has developed a program for young males who are siblings or who will become baby-sitters or fathers one day. "Guys Can Be Gentle Too" encourages male and female children to discuss and role play how girls *and* boys can care for and relate to young children. By challenging traditional male-female stereotypes about parenting, this program goes to the heart of many SBS and child abuse cases — male responses to stress. As a culture we encourage boys and men to be "tough"; we do not expect or teach them to be nurturing with children. And yet, clearly, young men are being put into child care situations for which they are unprepared, both in terms of personal maturity and social expectations. This male-oriented program in Utah is being taken to juvenile detention centers, prisons, schools, parenting classes, and anger management classes in an effort to convince caretakers that shaking is never an appropriate response to a crying child.

Since 1993, the American Academy of Pediatrics has endorsed the "Don't Shake the Baby" campaign conducted by the national organization SBS Prevention Plus, which includes a video, various educational print materials, and opportunities for training and consultation with experts in the field. If prevention programs such as these were incorporated all the way through high school health classes (which are required in most states) and were supported with consistent media messages about the dangers of shaking, we would have some of the most comprehensive preventative coverage available to us. This kind of campaign would require a mobilization of national resources and commitment on behalf of children and would generate sustained public conversation about individual and community responsibility that would help us change the way we protect our children.

I can't begin to address the complex economic and social dimensions implicated in a culture of child abuse. Moreover, abusing children is not an invention of the late twentieth century, and childhood, the experts tell us, is a relatively modern notion. In bygone centuries, children were treated as little adults, and often brutally so. It's only the last hundred years or so that have seen the notion of childhood emerge as a distinctive and precious phase of human development. But whatever the norms of centuries past, we know that our treatment of children is getting worse relative to our own times. According to the September 1996 study released by the U.S. Department of Health and Human Services, the abuse and neglect of America's young nearly doubled between 1986 and 1993. The estimated number of abused children rose to 2.81 million in 1993, up 98 percent from the 1986 report. These figures "herald a true rise in the scope and severity of child abuse and neglect in the United States."[10]

Where to begin? We must start by being willing to see what is happening to children around us and by speaking up on their behalf. This is more challenging than it might seem, for it is difficult to know when it is right to keep silent and when we are called to speak. "You got sucked right in," commented a lawyer friend regarding my involvement in Christopher's case. Immediately, I felt foolish. It seemed I hadn't the good sense to keep my distance and exercise an appropriate sense of proportion. Understandably, some professionals — doctors, lawyers, and social services workers, for example — must guard against emotional involvement with clients and patients or they would go crazy trying to share each burden of pain laid at their doorstep.

And yet, there comes a time when most of us will get called by something we can't explain, something that tells us it is time to heed the figure by the side of the road, whether it's practical, rewarding, or dangerous. The Scriptures tell us that God knows about even the tiny sparrow that falls to the earth. Although I'm skeptical about just how closely God is keeping track of things, I keep returning to a model of relationship that I think of as divinely ordained. We are called, not just to grand and heroic actions, but to ordinary actions of listening and sharing in whatever way is appropriate for us. Even if there were no religious resources at all for us to refer to, we would still be called to such things simply because it's the right thing to do.

Christopher's story is a call out of ourselves, a call to make that first motion, the primal gesture of human healing. Listening. Hearing. Seeing. Christopher was his own little person, unique, irreplaceable. But

10. A. Sedlak and Diane D. Broadhurst, *Executive Summary of the Third National Incidence Study of Child Abuse and Neglect* (NIS-3) (Washington, DC: U.S. Department of Health and Human Services, 1996), 17.

what happened to him was all too ordinary — not something that happens in a sordid slum in some distant, unspecified city to a child of a different race or class. No, like the subtle infusion of drugs into every small town and school in America, child abuse is now part of who we are as a culture. That is why this is a story of quiet horror, because it takes place in a way and a setting that could be any town, and many families. If we isolate Christopher's family with our denial or our self-righteous indignation, then we've made ourselves feel better at their expense, but we haven't done much of anything constructive. We cannot refuse to know his death; we must be willing to reach out, one child at a time, as we are called. And then we must speak and act.

Let's get the word out: Never, never, never shake a baby.

The Saturday after Christopher was killed, Charlie took Katie to Murphysboro Lake for a walk, and he saw Christopher. Christopher said to him, "I'll be waiting for you and Maw Maw at the top of the hill." Then he disappeared. I prayed and asked God if I could see him just one more time. One evening, very late because I couldn't sleep, I looked in the doorway of his room. There he was, sleeping on his bed. He never did sleep much on his tummy, and he was sleeping like he always did, on his back with his arms flung up over his head. I went to bend over and kiss him and he was gone.

Resources on Shaken Baby Syndrome and Child Abuse

Resources

ON SHAKEN BABY SYNDROME
AND CHILD ABUSE

The first National Conference on Shaken Baby Syndrome was held November 10–12, 1996, in Salt Lake City, sponsored by the National Center on Child Abuse and Neglect, the Independent Order of Foresters, Intermountain Health Care, the National Network on Shaken Baby Syndrome Prevention, the Child Abuse Prevention Council of Utah, and twenty-four other supporters. For more information about this conference, contact Dr. Jacy Showers, Conference Director, SBS Prevention Plus, 217 County Rd. 219, Florence, CO 81226, or Marilyn Sandberg, Conference Director, Child Abuse Prevention Center, 2955 Harrison Blvd., Suite #102, Ogden, UT 84403.

BOOKS AND ARTICLES

Alexander, Randell C., and Wilbur L. Smith. "Shaken Baby Syndrome." *Infants and Young Children* 10 (1998): 1–9.

American Academy of Pediatrics. "Shaken Baby Syndrome: Inflicted Cerebral Trauma." *Pediatrics* 92 (1993): 872–75.

Barnett, Ola W., Cindy L. Miller-Perrin, and Robin D. Perrin. *Family Violence Across the Lifespan.* Thousand Oaks, CA: Sage Publications, 1997.

Bass, M., R. E. Kravath, and L. Glass. "Death-Scene Investigation in Sudden Infant Death." *New England Journal of Medicine* 315 (July 1986): 100–5.

Billmire, Elaine M., and Patricia A. Myers. "Serious Head Injury in Infants: Accident or Abuse." *Pediatrics* 75 (1985): 340–42.

Bolton, Frank G., and Susan R. Bolton. *Working with Violent Families.* Newbury Park, CA: Sage, 1987.

Brandon, Karen. "State to Erase Play as Shaken Baby Cause." *Chicago Tribune,* August 26, 1993, 1.

Caffey, J. "On the Theory and Practice of Shaking Infants." *American Journal of Diseases of Children* 124 (1972): 161–69.

———. "The Whiplash Shaken Infant Syndrome." *Pediatrics* 54 (1974): 396–403.

Case, Mary E. S. "Head Injury in Child Abuse." In *Child Maltreatment: A Clinical Guide and Reference,* edited by James A. Monteleone and Armand E. Brodeur, 1:75–87. St. Louis: G. W. Medical Publishing, 1994.

"Debate Grows over Causes of Shaken Baby Syndrome." *Houston Chronicle,* June 27, 1993, sec. A, 5.

Firstman, Richard, and Jamie Talan. *The Death of Innocents: A True Story of Murder, Medicine, and High Stakes Science.* New York: Bantam, 1997.

Gil, David G. *Violence Against Children: Physical Child Abuse in the United States.* Cambridge, MA: Harvard University Press, 1970.

Graham, Michael. "The Role of the Medical Examiner in Fatal Child Abuse." In *Child Maltreatment: A Clinical Guide and Reference,* edited by James A. Monteleone and Armand E. Brodeur, 1:431–58. St. Louis: G. W. Medical Publishing, 1994.

Hanna, Janan. "'Shaken Baby' Death Ruled Manslaughter." *Chicago Tribune,* February 2, 1994, 1.

Kirschner, Robert H., and Harry L. Wilson. "Fatal Child Abuse: The Pathologist's Perspective." In *Child Abuse: Medical Diagnosis and Management,* edited by Robert M. Reece, 325–57. Philadelphia: Lea & Febiger, 1994.

Knapp, Ronald J. *Beyond Endurance: When a Child Dies.* New York: Schocken Books, 1986.

Levitt, Carolyn J., Wilbur L. Smith, and Randell C. Alexander. "Abusive Head Trauma." In *Child Abuse: Medical Diagnosis and Management,* edited by Robert M. Reece, 1–22. Philadelphia: Lea & Febiger, 1994.

Monteleone, James A., and Armand E. Brodeur. "Identifying, Interpreting, and Reporting Injuries." In *Child Maltreatment: A Clinical Guide and Reference,* 1:1–26. St. Louis: G. W. Medical Publishing, 1994.

Nashelsky, Marcus B., and Jay D. Dix. "The Time Interval Between Lethal Infant Shaking and the Onset of Symptoms." *American Journal of Forensic Medicine and Pathology* 16, no. 2 (1995): 154–57.

Rosoff, Barbara D. *The Worst Loss: How Families Heal from the Death of a Child*. New York: Henry Holt & Co., 1994.

Sedlak, A., and Diane D. Broadhurst. *Executive Summary of the Third National Incidence Study of Child Abuse and Neglect* (NIS-3). Washington, DC: U.S. Department of Health and Human Services, 1996.

Showers, Jacy. "'Don't Shake the Baby': The Effectiveness of a Prevention Program." *Child Abuse and Neglect* 16 (1992): 11–18.

———. *The National Conference on Shaken Baby Syndrome: A Medical, Legal, and Prevention Challenge*. Executive Summary. Alexandria, VA: National Association of Children's Hospitals and Related Institutions, n.d. For a copy of this summary, contact National Center on Child Abuse and Neglect, 1-800-FYI-3366.

———. "Shaken Baby Syndrome: The Problem and a Model for Prevention." *Children Today* 21 (1992): 34–37.

Starling, S. P., et al. "Abusive Head Trauma: The Relationship of Perpetrators to Their Victims." *Pediatrics* 95 (1995): 259–62.

U.S. Advisory Board on Child Abuse and Neglect. *A Nation's Shame: Fatal Child Abuse and Neglect in the United States*. Washington, DC: U.S. Department of Health and Human Services, 1995.

ORGANIZATIONS AND PROGRAMS

Guys Can Be Gentle Too. Stacy Iverson, Program Coordinator, or Robb Hall, Prevention Specialist, Utah Child Abuse Prevention Center, 29955 Harrison Blvd., Suite #102, Ogden, UT 84403.

Healthy Families America. The National Committee to Prevent Child Abuse. P.O. Box 2866, Chicago, IL, 1-800-CHILDREN.

Healthy Families Arizona. Rebecca Ruffner, Chair, Healthy Families Arizona Steering Committee, P.O. Box 432, Prescott, AZ 86302, 1-520-445-5038.

National Committee to Prevent Child Abuse, 332 S. Michigan Avenue, Suite 1600, Chicago, IL 60604, 1-312-663-3520. www.childabuse.org.

Parents of Murdered Children, Inc., 100 East Eighth Street, B-41, Cincinnati, OH 45202.

SBS Prevention Plus. For print information, contact 649 Main Street, Suite B, Groveport, OH 43125, 1-800-858-5222. For training or consultation, contact 217 County Rd. 219, Florence, CO 81226, 1-719-784-3330.

Ann-Janine Morey, the mother of two young children, is the director of the University Core Curriculum and a professor of English at Southern Illinois University at Carbondale, where she teaches American literature, religion and literature, and the Bible as literature. She has published numerous articles on women's fiction and religion and literature. Morey's second book was short-listed for the James Russell Lowell Prize of the Modern Language Association and nominated for the American Academy of Religion's Award for Excellence in Publications. Her first short story appeared in the summer 1997 issue of *spelunker flophouse*. Morey's current research focuses on how American women writers use the Scriptures in their fiction.